Denial Management Counseling

Workbook

Practical Exercises for Motivating Substance Abusers to Recover

By **Terence T. Gorski**
with **Stephen F. Grinstead**

Project Team: Terence T. Gorski, Stephen F. Grinstead, Arthur B. Trundy, Joseph E. Troiani, and Roland F. Williams

Notice of Proprietary Information

This document contains copyrighted and proprietary information of Terence T. Gorski and The CENAPS® Corporation. Its receipt or possession does not convey any right to reproduce it except for personal use in accordance with existing copyright laws. Reproducing this workbook or any part of it without the specific written authorization of Terence T. Gorski and The CENAPS® Corporation is strictly forbidden.

If your agency would like the rights to use any part of this material in its program, please refer the appropriate agency representative to The CENAPS® Corporation, 6147 Deltona Blvd., Spring Hill, FL 34606, (352) 596-8000; fax: (352) 596-8002 to discuss the arrangements necessary to make that possible. Web site: *www.cenaps.com* or e-mail: *info@cenaps.com*.

© 2000

Terence T. Gorski

Printed In the United States of America

ISBN 10: 0-8309-0850-1

ISBN 13: 978-0-8309-0850-9

For training contact:

The CENAPS® Corporation

6147 Deltona Blvd.

Spring Hill, FL 34606

Phone: (352) 596-8000

Acknowledgments

There are many people and organizations that deserve special acknowledgement for making this workbook possible. First, there is *Stephen F. Grinstead* of CENAPS West who helped me conceptualize and bring this workbook into its final form. Second is Joseph E. Troiani, my colleague and life-long friend, who completed extensive field testing with the Department of the Army and with his addiction classes at the Adler School of Professional Psychology in Chicago, IL. Third, there is Rick Glantz of Rhea Jacobson Management who both field tested the materials and helped me find the appropriate title for this workbook. Fourth is the CENAPS® training team who field-tested this course as instructors, including *Steve Grinstead, Roland Williams, Arthur Trundy,* and *Joseph E. Troiani.* Finally, Tresa Watson and Tina Lee, the staff of the CENAPS Central office, played a vital role in coordinating innumerable details and behind-the-scenes work that the field testing and publication of these materials required.

The clinical materials this workbook is based on was field tested in a three-day clinical skills training format twenty-six times by sixteen organizations involving over 750 experienced addiction and mental health therapists in the development process. Special acknowledgement needs to be given to the members of this nationwide team listed below:

1. **Academy of Health Sciences, Department of the Army, Fort Sam, TX**
   - *Trainer:* Joseph E. Troiani
   - *7 DMC Field Tests:* (#1) 5/19–21/98, (#2) 8/11–13/98, (#3) 1/12–14/99, (#4) 3/16–18/99, (#5) 6/8–10/99, (#6) 8/17–19/99, and (#7) 11/15–17/99 all in San Antonio, TX

2. **Bridge House, New Orleans, LA**
   - *Trainer:* Stephen F. Grinstead
   - *1 DMC Field Test:* 9/22–24/99 in New Orleans, LA

3. **CENAPS West, Cupertino, CA**
   - *Trainer:* Stephen F. Grinstead
   - *1 DMC Field Test Date:* 8/25–27/99 in San Francisco, CA

4. **Ernst Kennedy Center, Charleston, SC**
   - *Trainer:* Arthur B. Trundy
   - *2 DMC Field Test:* (#1) 8/25–27/99; and (#2) 5/15–17/00

5. **Family Counseling Services, Cortland, NY**
   - *Trainer:* Arthur B. Trundy
   - *1 DMC Field Test Date:* 11/01–03/99

6. **Maxey Training School, Detroit, MI**
   - *Trainer:* Roland F. Williams
   - *2 DMC Field Test Dates:* On (#1) 8/24–26/98, and (#2) 12/7–9/98 in Novi, MI

7. **New Sunrise Hospital, San Fidel, NM**
   - *Trainer:* Roland F. Williams
   - *1 DMC Field Test Date:* 9/21–23/99 in San Fidel, NM

8. **Resource Alliance Inc., San Jose, CA**
   - *Trainer:* Stephen F. Grinstead
   - *1 DMC Field Test:* 9/30–10/2/98 San Jose, CA

9. **Rhea Jacobson Management, Battle Ground, WA**
   - *Trainer:* Rick Glantz
   - *4 DMC Field Tests:* (#1) 11/2–4/99 in Phoenix, AZ; (#2) 10/18–20/99 in Laurel, MD; (#3) 9/27–29/99 in Columbus, OH, (#4) 4/13–15/99 in Phoenix, AZ.

10. **Walden House, Inc., San Francisco, CA**
    - *Trainer:* Stephen F. Grinstead
    - *1 DMC Field Test Date:* 5/5–7/00 in San Francisco

11. **Washington Department of Corrections (WADOC), Airway Heights, WA**
    - *Trainer:* Terence T. Gorski
    - *1 DMC Field Test Date:* 4/20–22/99 in Spokane, WA

12. **Westbrook Health Services, Parkersberg, WV**
    - *Trainer:* Arthur B. Trundy
    - *1 DMC Field Test Date:* 1/26–28/00 in Parkersberg, WV

13. **Alameda City Health Services Agency, Oakland, CA**
    - *Trainer:* Roland F. Williams
    - *1 DMC Field Test:* 7/27/99 in Alameda, CA

14. **Alert Driving, Inc., San Jose, CA**
    - *Trainer:* Stephen F. Grinstead
    - *1 DMC Field Test Date:* 1/15/99 in San Jose, CA

15. **Community Treatment Center, Detroit, MI**
    - *Trainer:* Roland F. Williams
    - *1 DMC Field Test Date:* 10/12/99 in Detroit, MI

16. **High Intensity Drug Trafficking Area (HIDTA), Washington D.C.**
    - *Trainer:* Terence T. Gorski
    - *1 DMC Field Test Date:* 11/17/99 in Washington D.C.

Contents

Notice of Proprietary Information 2
Acknowledgments 3
Contents 5
The Goals of the Denial Management Workbook 7
    How to Use This Workbook 7
    Deciding How You Will Participate 8
    How This Workbook Is Structured 8
    Deciding to Face the Truth 10
    Your First Denial Management Exercise 11

Exercise #1: Understanding Denial as a Part of the Human Condition 12
    Exercise 1-1: The Need to Search for the Truth 13
    Exercise 1-2: The Tendency to Make Mistakes 15
    Exercise 1-3: The Tendency to Lie to Ourselves 18
    Exercise 1-4: The Tendency to Lie to Others 20
    Exercise 1-5: Denial as a Normal Defense Against Pain, Guilt, & Shame ... 22

Exercise #2: Understanding the Principles of Denial Management 25
    Exercise 2-1: The Benefits and Disadvantages of Using Denial 26
    Exercise 2-2: Acceptance and Problem Solving as Antidotes for Denial ... 29
    Exercise 2-3: Denial Can Be Recognized and Managed 32
    Exercise 2-4: Defining Denial in a Way that Can Help Manage It 34
    Exercise 2-5: The Feelings that Drive Denial 37

Exercise #3: Recognizing Your Denial Patterns 39
    Exercise 3-1: Reviewing the Denial Pattern Checklist 40
    Exercise 3-2: Learning How to Personalize Denial Patterns 52
    Exercise 3-3: Selecting the Denial Patterns You Tend to Use 54
    Exercise 3-4: Personalizing the First Denial Pattern You Selected 55
    Exercise 3-5: Personalizing the Second Denial Pattern You Selected 56
    Exercise 3-6: Personalizing the Third Denial Pattern You Selected 57

Exercise #4: Managing Denial 58
    Exercise 4-1: Managing the First Denial Pattern You Selected 61
    Exercise 4-2: Managing the Second Denial Pattern You Selected 63
    Exercise 4-3: Managing the Third Denial Pattern You Selected 65
    Exercise 4-4: Bringing Your Denial Management Skills Together 67

Exercise #5: Stopping Denial as You Think about Your Problems 70
    Exercise 5-1: The Problems that Caused You to Seek Help 71
    Exercise 5-2: The Relationship of Your Problems to Alcohol and Drug Use ... 72
    Exercise 5-3: The Consequences of Continued Alcohol or Drug Use 75
    Exercise 5-4: Pulling It All Together 78

Exercise #6: Stopping Denial as You Think about Your Life History 81

Exercise #7: Stopping Denial as You Think about Your Addiction Symptoms....... 85
Exercise #8: Stopping Denial as You Decide What to Do Next 90
Exercise #9: Evaluating Your Denial Management Skills 91
A Final Word... 94
Appendix #1: Abstinence Contract 95
Appendix #2: DMC Model Treatment Plan 96

The Goals of the Denial Management Workbook

This workbook is designed for people who have experienced problems related to the use of alcohol and other drugs, but who honestly believe that they are not addicted and do not need treatment.

If you are starting this workbook, you have probably been forced to seek help by circumstances beyond your control. Maybe you sought help to avoid negative consequences such as getting fired, divorced, or losing your children. You may have come up positive in a random alcohol or drug test at work or at school. Some of you may have been arrested for alcohol and drug-related crimes such as driving under the influence, possessing or selling illegal drugs, or committing other crimes to get money to buy alcohol or drugs. Some of you sought help because you wanted to stop the pain and problems that go along with drinking and drugging. Some of you are under correctional supervision as a result of alcohol- and drug-related offenses and are hoping to get a shorter sentence, to qualify for parole, or to please your probation or parole officer.

No matter what forced you to start this process, you are probably angry. You probably have a battle going on inside between two parts of yourself: the addictive self and the sober self.

The *addictive self* is the part of you that doesn't want to think or talk about your alcohol or drug use. The addictive self resents the fact that you are being forced to complete this workbook. Your addictive self believes that you don't have problems, or that your problems just aren't as bad as people say that they are. You addictive self is telling you that you have good reasons for using alcohol and/or other drugs, that it's not your fault that you were referred into treatment, and someone else is to blame for your problems. This addictive part of you believes you won't learn anything by completing this workbook because you are not addicted. This addictive part of you truly believes you are a social drinker and/or a recreational drug user and that you definitely do not need help.

The *sober self* is the part of you that thinks you might have a problem with alcohol or drugs and wants to do something about it. This is the truth seeking part of you that wants to know what's really going on so you can figure out the best way to handle it.

Most people starting this workbook are well acquainted with the addictive self. They have little or no knowledge of the sober self because they have spent a great deal of time and energy pushing the sober self out of the way so they could go on "enjoying" their alcohol and drug use without having to deal with their problems.

How to Use This Workbook

Learning how to recognize and manage your own denial will require more than just reading this workbook and filling out the exercises. You'll need to discuss your responses to each exercise with other people who can help you sort out the thoughts and feelings that get stirred up. We strongly recommend that one of these people be a therapist or counselor trained in the CENAPS® Model of Relapse Prevention. You can get a list of Certified Relapse Prevention Specialists by calling or writing to The CENAPS® Corporation, 6147 Deltona Blvd, Spring Hill, FL 34606, (352) 596-8000 or by visiting their Web site at *www.cenaps.com* or *www.relapse.org*.

If you get stuck anywhere in the process you can go to our website: *www.cenaps.com* and/ or send an e-mail to *info@cenaps.com*. One of the certified specialists will be available to respond to your questions.

If you don't have a therapist, you can do these exercises with the assistance of a self-help group sponsor who is willing and able to support you through this process. It's also a good idea to supplement your individual sessions with group sessions where each group member is working through these exercises at the same time. *Discussing what you're learning from each exercise with another person or a group of people will improve your ability to change in a way that will prevent relapse.*

Deciding How You Will Participate

The first decision that you have to make is whether or not you are willing to complete the exercises in this workbook and discuss what you learned about yourself with a counselor, therapist, or self-help group sponsor. There are several different ways in which you can deal with the completion of the exercises in this workbook.

1. *You can refuse to do it.* This would probably mean that you would have to suffer the consequences that you entered this program in order to avoid.

2. *You can skate through the process by withholding information and telling lies.* If you do this, you will miss a valuable opportunity to get some answers about what is really going wrong in your life and what you can do to fix it.

3. *You can actively and honestly participate.* By doing this you can make the best use of time and open up the possibility that you might get some significant benefits from going through the process.

I certainly hope you choose to actively and honestly participate in this process even though a big part of you doesn't want to. If you do, I can assure you that you will learn more about yourself and how to deal with what is really going on in your life than you ever could have imagined.

How This Workbook Is Structured

This workbook is divided into nine exercises. Each exercise will explain some basic information about denial management and then ask you to answer a series of questions that will help you apply that information to your current situation. Here is a brief summary of each exercise.

Exercise #1: Understanding Denial as a Part of the Human Condition: This exercise explains that denial is a normal and natural part of the human condition. Denial is related to our need to search for the truth about what is happening to us despite our tendency to make mistakes. Whether we like to admit it or not, we all have fragile egos that can be easily hurt when we make mistakes. This creates the tendency for us to lie to ourselves when we do make mistakes in order to avoid the pain. We are all capable of convincing ourselves that the lies that we tell ourselves are in fact true. Once we start believing our own lies, we tend to become deceptive and can start lying to others whether we mean to or not. As a result, we all need to develop personal and social systems for finding the truth while protecting ourselves from self-deception and the lies of others. Denial management is a personal system for finding the truth while protecting yourself from self-deception.

Exercise #2: Understanding the Principles of Denial Management: This exercise explains the basic information needed to understand and recognize denial so you can make a choice between continuing to lie to yourself or facing and dealing with the truth. Denial is the natural tendency to avoid the pain that is caused by thinking and talking about serious problems. This pain is avoided by using a set of automatic and unconscious thoughts, feelings, and actions that keep us from thinking and talking about our problems. Denial is a normal psychological defense that has both benefits and disadvantages. The major benefit of using denial is that it allows us to avoid feeling the pain caused by serious or overwhelming problems. The major disadvantage is that it prevents us from seeing what is really going on and effectively managing our problems. Fortunately, there are two antidotes for denial—accepting the truth about what is going wrong with our lives, and developing effective problem-solving strategies to address our problems. The primary feelings that drive denial are pain, anger, fear, guilt, and shame. Denial can be recognized. You can face the truth about what is happening in your life, and by doing this you can turn your life around.

Exercise #3: Recognizing Your Denial Patterns: This exercise describes twelve common denial patterns that people tend to use to deny that they have serious problems with alcohol or other drugs. You will be asked to review a denial pattern checklist that explains these denial patterns and to select and personalize the three denial patterns that you tend to use most often.

Exercise #4: Managing Denial: This exercise shows you how to stop denial by identifying and managing the thoughts, feelings, urges, actions, and social reactions that drive the denial process.

Exercise #5: Stopping Denial as You Think about Your Problems: This exercise will test your ability to recognize and manage your own denial as you think and talk about the problems that caused you to start using this workbook. First you will be asked to describe the problems that brought you to treatment. Then you will be asked to look at the relationship of your problems to alcohol and drug use and the potential consequences, both good and bad, of continuing to use alcohol or other drugs. You will then be asked to tie all of this information together in your mind, look at the big picture of what is happening at this moment in your life, and make a hard decision about what you want to do about your problems. At each step in this process, you will be asked to notice if you were able to recognize and stop your denial when it was turned on.

Exercise #6: Stopping Denial as You Think about Your Life History: In this exercise you will be asked to review the important things that have happened to you in the course of your life and think about how alcohol and drugs were related to each of the key life events. At each step in this process, you will be asked to notice if you were able to recognize and stop your denial when it was turned on.

Exercise #7: Stopping Denial as You Think about Your Addiction Symptoms: In this exercise you will review the common symptoms of substance abuse and dependence and be asked to decide if each symptom applies to you. You will then be able to tie all of your answers together and see if you meet medical criteria for substance abuse or dependence or at high risk of developing it. At each step in this process, you will be asked to notice if you were able to recognize and stop your denial when it was turned on.

Exercise #8: Stopping Denial as You Decide What to Do Next: In this exercise you will be asked to decide what you are going to do next. You can decide to stay in denial and pretend your problems don't exist or you can decide to recognize you problems and enter appropriate treatment so you can learn to effectively manage your alcohol and drug problems and get your life back on track.

Exercise #9: Evaluating Your Denial Management Skills: In this exercise you will evaluate how well you learned the skills needed to recognize and manage your denial.

Learning to identify and manage your denial is not easy, but it is a necessary first step in learning how to recover from serious alcohol and drug problems. Learning to manage your denial will require hard work and a willingness to use each exercise in this workbook as a tool for self-examination and self-change. It will also require you to apply the skills while looking at the problems that forced you into treatment, examining your life and addiction history, and evaluating the addiction symptoms that you have experienced. *You can recover*. Learning how to manage your denial will help.

Deciding to Face the Truth

Let's face a difficult fact—if everything were going well in your life, you wouldn't be reading this workbook. The fact that you are reading this workbook should tell you that something isn't working in your life. Somehow you put yourself in the position where others are calling the shots and forcing you to do something that you really don't want to do. How did you put yourself in this one-down position?

I don't know the answer to this question. Chances are that, at this moment, you don't know the answer either. But I am sure of three things: First, if you don't know the answer to this question, it probably means that your denial is making it impossible for you to see the truth; Second, if you don't go through the process of finding the honest answer to this question for yourself, you will probably continue to get trapped into doing things you don't want to do; Third, and most important, if you don't figure out what's really going on and learn more effective ways to deal with it, things will probably keep getting worse.

This workbook will help you find out the truth about what is going wrong in your life. It will help you to look at your problems and to see how they are related to alcohol and other drugs. Most importantly, this workbook will help you see what you need to do to build a better life for yourself and those you love.

You have a hard decision to make. It would be best if you made this decision consciously and deliberately. The decision is this: *Are you willing to face the truth about what is happening to you and act accordingly?*

If your decision is "yes," this workbook, along with your counselor, treatment program, and self-help group can help you. If your decision is "no," you are probably condemning yourself to experience ongoing problems that could destroy you and those you love. The choice is yours. Choose wisely.

Your First Denial Management Exercise

Take a few moments to answer the following questions:

1. If you are using this workbook, you are probably being forced to look at your use of alcohol and drugs and a big part of you really doesn't want to do that. Somehow, you've gotten into serious trouble and someone has told you to stop drinking and/or drugging or to suffer some consequences that you want to avoid. If this is true, *how did you allow this to happen?*

   _____
   _____
   _____
   _____

2. Are you willing to do whatever is necessary to solve the problems that you are facing so you can deal with your life in a sober and responsible way?

   ☐ Yes ☐ No ☐ Unsure ☐ Unwilling to say Explain your answer below:

   _____
   _____
   _____
   _____

3. Are you willing to make a commitment to complete all of the exercises in this workbook as honestly as you can and discuss your answers in therapy or with members of your self-help group?

   ☐ Yes ☐ No ☐ Unsure Explain your answer below:

   _____
   _____
   _____

Exercise #1: Understanding Denial as a Part of the Human Condition

This exercise explains that denial is a normal and natural part of the human condition.

1. Denial is related to our need to search for the truth about what is happening to us despite of our tendency to make mistakes.

2. Whether we like to admit it or not, we all can be easily hurt when we make mistakes.

3. When we do make mistakes, our fear of being hurt creates the tendency to lie to ourselves in order to avoid pain, guilt, and shame.

4. We are all capable of convincing ourselves that the lies we tell ourselves are, in fact, true.

5. Once we start believing our own lies, we tend to start lying to others whether we mean to or not.

6. Denial is a normal and natural response to experiencing serious life problems.

7. Even though most people try to be honest, we all have the human tendency to make mistakes.

8. Once we make a mistake, the fear of experiencing pain, guilt, and shame creates a tendency to lie to ourselves and others about the mistakes.

9. This can lead to the habitual use of denial to avoid experiencing the pain, guilt, and shame.

10. This means that denial is the natural tendency to avoid the pain, guilt, and shame that is caused by thinking and talking about serious problems.

11. Denial is a set of automatic and unconscious thoughts, feelings, and actions that keep us from thinking and talking about our problems in order to avoid pain, guilt, and shame.

Exercise 1-1: The Need to Search for the Truth

As human beings we are all truth-seeking animals. Most of us want to know what's really going on in our lives. This tendency to look for the truth makes us ask ourselves questions like:

- Who Am I?
- Why am I here?
- How do I fit in?
- What is my place in the world?
- What does the world require of me in order to survive and thrive?

When things go wrong or we experience frustration, pain, or disappointment we ask more questions like:

- What is wrong with me?
- How can I get well?
- What can I do to solve my problems?
- What can I do to stop my pain and suffering?
- What can I do to live a life that is meaningful to me?

Read the following statements and ask yourself how strongly you agree or disagree with each one. Then briefly explain each answer.

1. I want to know the truth about what is happening in my life.

    ☐ A. Strongly Agree ☐ B. Agree ☐ C. Disagree ☐ D. Strongly Disagree

    Explain your answer: _____
    _____
    _____

2. I have spent time trying to answer questions like *Who Am I? Why am I here? How do I fit in? What is my place in the world? What does the world require of me in order to survive and thrive?*

    ☐ A. Strongly Agree ☐ B. Agree ☐ C. Disagree ☐ D. Strongly Disagree

    Explain your answer: _____
    _____
    _____

3. Things have happened in my life that have caused me to ask myself *What is wrong with me?*

    ☐ A. Strongly Agree ☐ B. Agree ☐ C. Disagree ☐ D. Strongly Disagree

    Explain your answer: _____
    _____
    _____

4. I am interested in figuring out what I must do to solve my problems, stop my pain and suffering, and live a life that is meaningful me.

   ☐ A. Strongly Agree ☐ B. Agree ☐ C. Disagree ☐ D. Strongly Disagree

   Explain your answer: _____
   _____
   _____

5. **Denial Check:** Answer the following questions to see if your denial might have been activated during this exercise

   A. Did your stress go up as you completed this exercise?

   ☐ Yes ☐ No ☐ Unsure ☐ Unwilling to say

   Explain your answer:_____
   _____
   _____

   B. Did an inner conflict or argument start in your head as you completed this exercise?

   ☐ Yes ☐ No ☐ Unsure ☐ Unwilling to say

   Explain your answer:_____
   _____
   _____

   C. Did you feel an urge to avoid answering the questions or to tell lies or half truths?

   ☐ Yes ☐ No ☐ Unsure ☐ Unwilling to say

   Explain your answer:_____
   _____
   _____

**Unfortunately, no matter how hard we try, we don't always find the truth.
Go to the next part of the exercise to find out why.**

Exercise 1-2: The Tendency to Make Mistakes

As human beings, we are fallible. We are not perfect. We tend to make mistakes. The following exercise will help you understand why we tend to make mistakes. Read each item carefully and answer the questions that follow it.

The truth is hard to find: The real world is a confusing place that does not come with an instruction manual. We have to figure out how things work and that's not easy. Even well-trained scientists who are using the most advanced scientific equipment make honest mistakes in explaining the truth about the world around them. Mankind has spent thousands of years trying to learn the truth about the world. Yet every day we are learning new things and correcting mistakes that, only yesterday, we thought were the truth.

We learn about the world from other people who might be wrong: Our first teachers are usually our parents or caretakers who, like the rest of us, are fallible human beings. As a result, they may fail to teach us some things we need to know. They may also teach us things which they believe are true, that, in fact, are not. At times, they may deliberately lie to us.

We are programmed to learn by trial and error, so we must periodically make mistakes in order to learn: Learning by trial and error works like this. We hear something or see someone do something. It seems like a good idea, so we try it for ourselves. Sometimes what we try works and sometimes it doesn't. Either way we learn from the consequences of what we do. If we try something and it works for us we tend to keep doing it. If we try something and it doesn't work for us, we tend to stop doing it and try something else. Mistakes are a normal and natural part of the process.

We confuse feeling good with knowing the truth: We can use emotional reasoning by making the mistake of believing "If something makes me *feel good*, it must be good for me!" We can also make another mistake by believing "If something makes me *feel bad*, it must be bad for me!"

We get set in our ways, refuse to admit that we are wrong, and keep doing things that don't work. We can easily believe that something "should work" even when it doesn't. Because we can't handle being wrong, we tend to keep trying the same things and making the same mistake over and over again. There is an old saying that goes, *Insanity is expecting different consequences from the same behavior*.

Answer the following questions to apply the information that you just read.

1. I believe the world can be a confusing place and that the truth can be difficult to find.

    ☐ A. Strongly Agree   ☐ B. Agree   ☐ C. Disagree   ☐ D. Strongly Disagree

    Explain your answer: _____

    _____

2. I believe we learn about the world from other people who might be wrong.

    ☐ A. Strongly Agree   ☐ B. Agree   ☐ C. Disagree   ☐ D. Strongly Disagree

    Explain your answer: _____

    _____

    _____

3. I believe we are programmed to learn by trial and error so we must periodically make mistakes in order to learn.

☐ A. Strongly Agree ☐ B. Agree ☐ C. Disagree ☐ D. Strongly Disagree

Explain your answer: _____

_____

_____

4. I sometimes confuse feeling good with knowing the truth, and feeling bad with not knowing what is true.

☐ A. Strongly Agree ☐ B. Agree ☐ C. Disagree ☐ D. Strongly Disagree

Explain your answer: _____

_____

_____

5. I get set in my ways, refuse to admit that I am wrong, and keep doing things that don't work.

☐ A. Strongly Agree ☐ B. Agree ☐ C. Disagree ☐ D. Strongly Disagree

Explain your answer: _____

_____

_____

6. **Denial Check:** Answer the following questions to see if your denial might have been activated during this exercise

   A. Did your stress go up as you completed this exercise?

   ☐ Yes ☐ No ☐ Unsure ☐ Unwilling to say

   Explain your answer: _____

   _____

   _____

   B. Did an inner conflict or argument start in your head as you completed this exercise?

   ☐ Yes ☐ No ☐ Unsure ☐ Unwilling to say

   Explain your answer: _____

   _____

   _____

C. Did you feel an urge to avoid answering the questions or to tell lies or half truths?

☐ Yes ☐ No ☐ Unsure ☐ Unwilling to say

Explain your answer:_____

_____

_____

**Even though we are fallible, it is difficult for us to admit our mistakes.
Go to the next part of the exercise to find out why.**

Exercise 1-3: The Tendency to Lie to Ourselves

Most of us have a tendency to lie to ourselves. There are two reasons for this:

We prefer to see things in a way that causes the least pain and gives us the easiest solution or way out: Wanting to take the easy way out is a normal and natural tendency in every human being. As a result, we all have a natural tendency to see things in a way that causes us the least pain and gives us the easiest solution or way out. People who succeed learn to recognize that this desire for the easy way out is a defect of character or a self-defeating personality trait that needs to be overcome. Whenever they find themselves wanting to take the easier, softer way, they see it as a warning sign that they are setting themselves up to get into trouble.

We can start believing our own lies: Some people call this being *sincerely deluded*—we believe in the truth of our point of view in spite of overwhelming and undeniable evidence that we are wrong. We are not actually lying to ourselves. We just don't care about the evidence because our minds are made up. We confuse the way we want things to be with the way that things really are. Once we develop "the truth as I see it" we tend to defend and protect that truth, especially when others try to show us that it might be wrong. When we believe our own lies, we can't tell what the truth is because we believe that our lies really are the truth.

Answer the following questions to apply the information that you just read.

1. At times I prefer to see things in a way that causes me the least pain and gives me the easiest solution or way out.

   ☐ A. Strongly Agree ☐ B. Agree ☐ C. Disagree ☐ D. Strongly Disagree

   Explain your answer: _____
   _____
   _____

2. There have been times in my life when I have told myself a lie and then started to believe that my own lies were true.

   ☐ A. Strongly Agree ☐ B. Agree ☐ C. Disagree ☐ D. Strongly Disagree

   Explain your answer: _____
   _____
   _____

3. How do you currently test your beliefs to determine if they are actually true or if you are lying to yourself?

   _____
   _____
   _____

4. **Denial Check:** Answer the following questions to see if your denial might have been activated during this exercise

    A. Did your stress go up as you completed this exercise?

    ☐ Yes ☐ No ☐ Unsure ☐ Unwilling to say

    Explain your answer:_____
    _____
    _____

    B. Did an inner conflict or argument start in your head as you completed this exercise?

    ☐ Yes ☐ No ☐ Unsure ☐ Unwilling to say

    Explain your answer:_____
    _____
    _____

    C. Did you feel an urge to avoid answering the questions or to tell lies or half truths?

    ☐ Yes ☐ No ☐ Unsure ☐ Unwilling to say

    Explain your answer:_____
    _____
    _____

**Not only do we lie to ourselves, we also have a tendency to lie to others.
Go to the next exercise to find out why.**

Exercise 1-4: The Tendency to Lie to Others

Sometimes we can consciously and deliberately lie to others. This is called *deceit*. We are most likely to lie to others when we feel threatened because something bad could happen to us or because we believe that lying is the best way to get something that we want.

1. Have you ever consciously and deliberately lied to other people?

   ☐ Yes ☐ No ☐ Unsure ☐ Unwilling to say

   If yes, describe a situation when you deliberately lied to someone else.

   _____
   _____
   _____

2. Have you ever lied to others because you felt threatened or believed something bad would happen to you if you told the truth?

   ☐ Yes ☐ No ☐ Unsure ☐ Unwilling to say

   If yes, describe a situation when you deliberately lied to someone else to keep something bad from happening.

   _____
   _____
   _____

3. Have you ever lied in order to get something you wanted?

   ☐ Yes ☐ No ☐ Unsure ☐ Unwilling to say

   If yes, describe a situation when you deliberately lied to get something you wanted.

   _____
   _____
   _____

4. Do you believe lying can help you get what you want out of your treatment?

   ☐ Yes ☐ No ☐ Unsure ☐ Unwilling to say

   Explain your answer: _____
   _____
   _____
   _____

5. **Denial Check:** Answer the following questions to see if your denial might have been activated during this exercise

   A. Did your stress go up as you completed this exercise?

   ☐ Yes ☐ No ☐ Unsure ☐ Unwilling to say

   Explain your answer: _____

   _____

   _____

   B. Did an inner conflict or argument start in your head as you completed this exercise?

   ☐ Yes ☐ No ☐ Unsure ☐ Unwilling to say

   Explain your answer: _____

   _____

   _____

   C. Did you feel an urge to avoid answering the questions or to tell lies or half truths?

   ☐ Yes ☐ No ☐ Unsure ☐ Unwilling to say

   Explain your answer: _____

   _____

   _____

**The next part of this exercise will show that
denial is a normal and natural defense against pain, guilt, and shame.**

Exercise 1-5: Denial as a Normal Defense Against Pain, Guilt, and Shame

Denial is a normal and natural psychological defense. Just as the human body has an immune system to protect it from dangerous physical organisms, the human mind has a *mental immune system* to protect it from overwhelming pain and problems. That mental immune system is called *a psychological defense system*. The goal of this psychological defense system is to protect the integrity of our mind and personality.

Denial is one part of this defensive system. It is activated whenever we are asked to think or talk about a painful or overwhelming problem. There is nothing sick, pathological, or wrong about this. Denial is a normal and natural human response to severe pain and problems.

Everyone uses denial every day. The brain has an automatic screening system called the Reticular Activating System (RAS) that forces it to block out certain perceptions that it is programmed to consider irrelevant. In states of normal stress, the brain locks on to signals that have *pay value* (this is good for me) or *threat value* (this is bad for me). Everything else gets blocked out or unconsciously denied.

Our brain is programmed by the *values* that are integrated into our personality. *Values* are the things that we think are important enough to invest time, energy, and resources to acquire and maintain. Our brain is programmed to notice anything we have assigned value to. If we assign it a positive value, we can say the perception has "pay value" and the brain says "This is good for me! I want it!" The perception is presented to the conscious mind along with the emotional urge to go get it.

The brain is also programmed to notice anything that challenges or threatens our values. These things have "threat value" and the brain says "this is bad for me. I must get away from this or destroy it." So the perception is noticed and presented to the mind along with an emotional urge to get away from or destroy the threat.

The emotional urge to get away from the threat is called "fear". *Fear* ranges in intensity from mild anxiety to intense panic. The emotional urge to destroy the threat is called "anger." *Anger* ranges in intensity from mild frustration to intense rage. *Violence* is the behavioral response to intense anger processed through a mistaken belief that "violence is an effective way to deal with this threat."

At times of high stress the brain can get emotionally overloaded. At these times the brain will activate automatic defenses, which we will call denial patterns. Each denial pattern is turned on by a specific trigger that threatens something that we value. As a severe problem causes intense stress, the brain turns on intense fear and/or anger. This activates a psychological program that starts mobilizing automatic defensive thoughts and the urge to use resistant behaviors.

These defensive reactions are normal and natural. Anyone who has a serious problem or illness will tend to deny it. People with good sobriety and mental health skills will learn how to recognize and stop the denial early, before the denial causes serious problems.

Let's personalize this information by imagining the following situations and answering some questions about how we might respond:

1. *Imagine yourself in this situation. You are at work and suddenly begin to feel a pain in your chest. At first the pain isn't very bad, but it slowly starts to get worse. The pain keeps getting worse and worse.*

    A. How bad would the pain have to get for you to consider your chest pain to be a serious problem?

    _____
    _____
    _____

    B. How bad would the pain have to get for you to ask someone to call an ambulance because you are having a heart attack?

    _____
    _____
    _____

    C. Do you think you might deny the pain and try to tough it out until you couldn't work or collapsed on the job?

    ☐ Yes ☐ No ☐ Unsure ☐ Unwilling to say.

    Explain your answer: _____
    _____
    _____
    _____

2. *Imagine yourself in this situation:* You believe you are a social drinker or a recreational drug user. You honestly don't believe you have any problems with your alcohol or drug use. Things start going wrong in your life, but you are convinced they have nothing to do with drinking or drugging. Things keep getting worse and people you know start telling you that your problems are caused by your drinking and drugging. You don't believe them. You do your best to solve your problems but keep on drinking socially and using drugs recreationally.

    A. How bad would things have to get for you to consider you might have a drinking or drug problem?

    _____
    _____
    _____
    _____

B. How bad would things have to get for you to ask for help with your alcohol or drug problem?

_____
_____
_____
_____

C. Do you think you might deny the pain and problems caused by your alcohol and drug use and try to tough it out until you lost your friends, hurt your family, lost your job, or got sent to jail?

☐ Yes ☐ No ☐ Unsure ☐ Unwilling to say

Explain your answer: _____
_____
_____
_____

3. **Denial Check:** Answer the following questions to see if your denial might have been activated during this exercise:

   A. Did your stress go up as you completed this exercise?

   ☐ Yes ☐ No ☐ Unsure ☐ Unwilling to say

   Explain your answer:_____
   _____
   _____

   B. Did an inner conflict or argument start in your head as you completed this exercise?

   ☐ Yes ☐ No ☐ Unsure ☐ Unwilling to say

   Explain your answer:_____
   _____
   _____

   C. Did you feel an urge to avoid answering the questions or to tell lies or half truths?

   ☐ Yes ☐ No ☐ Unsure ☐ Unwilling to say

   Explain your answer:_____
   _____
   _____

This exercise stops here. Relax and take a break.

Exercise #2: Understanding the Principles of Denial Management

This exercise explains the basic information needed to understand and recognize denial so you can make a choice between continuing to lie to yourself or facing and dealing with the truth.

1. Denial is a normal psychological defense that has both benefits and disadvantages.
2. The major benefit of using denial is that it allows us to avoid feeling the pain caused by serious or overwhelming problems.
3. The major disadvantage is that it prevents us from seeing what is really going on and effectively managing our problems.
4. Fortunately, there are two antidotes for denial: accepting the truth about what is going wrong with our lives and developing effective problem solving strategies to address our problems.
5. The primary feelings that drive denial are pain, anger, fear, guilt, and shame.
6. Denial and the feelings that drive it can be recognized and effectively managed.
7. We can face the truth about what is happening in our lives, and by doing so, turn our lives around.

**Because denial can hurt us, why would we keep using it?
The next part of this exercise will show that using denial
has both benefits and disadvantages.**

Exercise 2-1: The Benefits and Disadvantages of Using Denial

There are both benefits and disadvantages to using denial. The benefits make us want to keep using denial despite of the disadvantages that we tend to experience.

The Benefits of Denial

The major benefit of using denial is that it helps us to deal with unbearable pain and overwhelming problems. If you don't believe it, talk to people who were near death as a result of a serious illness or injury and then survived. Ask them if at their worst moment they realized how sick and close to death they were. Most people will tell you they didn't. It was only as they began getting well that they realized how sick they really were. Why? Because at the moment of greatest illness, denial can be very strong and help us to keep hope alive by preventing us from seeing how hopeless the situation is.

You can also see the use of denial when talking with people who have a run a twenty-six-mile marathon. Somewhere around twenty miles, most runners find that there body rebels and threatens to shut down. This is called hitting the wall. Experienced runners get through "the wall" by using denial. They try to ignore the real physical pain they are experiencing and focus on getting through the wall and completing the race. Does it work? Sometimes it does. Don't forget, however, that even the most experienced marathon runners have collapsed because the denial of their exhaustion caused them to push themselves beyond their physical endurance. In these cases the benefits that denial provides by helping deal with intense pain is outweighed by the disadvantages—the inability to accurately assess the truth of a given situation.

The Disadvantages of Denial

The major disadvantage of denial is that it prevents us from seeing what is wrong and taking appropriate action to handle the situation. As a result our problems can get worse in the long run because we refuse to recognize what is wrong and to do what is necessary to handle the problem.

When I was about ten years old my father had a friend named Al who had serious diabetes. Al refused to change his diet, manage his stress, or take his insulin. Why? Because Al was convinced the doctor was wrong. He didn't believe he had diabetes. In his mind he had a circulatory problem that had nothing to do with the amount of sugar he was eating. According to Al, the crazy doctors didn't know what they were talking about. He refused to manage his diabetes and kept getting sicker. Before he died, both of his arms and legs were amputated because of his "circulation problem." Right up until his death, however, Al insisted he did not have diabetes. His diabetes would have been manageable if only he could have learned to manage his denial.

Denial Blocks Recognition and Problem Solving

As you can see, denial prevents us from seeing what is wrong and doing what needs to be done to solve the problem. If we don't learn how to recognize and manage denial, it will prevent us from recognizing and solving important problems. Denial of a problem can create more serious consequences than the problem itself. Denial, a normal and natural defense mechanism designed to protect us from pain and problems, can backfire and cause us to experience more pain and problems.

Here are some examples:

- The person who didn't have problems with his marriage because of his drinking and drugging came home one day to an empty house because his wife left with his children and started the divorce proceedings.
- The person who was an excellent employee with an unreasonable boss was suddenly fired and couldn't understand why.
- The person convicted of his third time for driving under the influence of alcohol couldn't understand why the judge was sending him to jail.

Let's look at how this information applies to you by answering the following questions.

1. What are three benefits you could get from denying the problems that made you start using this workbook?

   A. Benefit #1: _____

   B. Benefit #2: _____

   C. Benefit #3: _____

2. What are three disadvantages or problems you could get from denying the problems that made you start using this workbook?

   A. Problem #1: _____

   B. Problem #2: _____

   C. Problem #3: _____

3. Did you ever suddenly get in trouble and not understand why, only to discover later that your problem was obvious to everyone except you?

   ☐ Yes ☐ No ☐ Unsure ☐ Unwilling to say

   Describe the situation: _____
   _____
   _____

4. **Denial Check:** Answer the following questions to see if your denial might have been activated during this exercise

   A. Did your stress go up as you completed this exercise?

   ☐ Yes ☐ No ☐ Unsure ☐ Unwilling to say

   Explain your answer: _____

   _____

   _____

   B. Did an inner conflict or argument start in your head as you completed this exercise?

   ☐ Yes ☐ No ☐ Unsure ☐ Unwilling to say

   Explain your answer: _____

   _____

   _____

   C. Did you feel an urge to avoid answering the questions or to tell lies or half truths?

   ☐ Yes ☐ No ☐ Unsure ☐ Unwilling to say

   Explain your answer: _____

   _____

   _____

**If denial is a poison that affects our mind, is there an antidote?
Go to the next part of this exercise to find out.**

Exercise 2-2: Acceptance and Problem Solving As Antidotes for Denial

Fortunately there are two antidotes for denial: acceptance and problem solving.

Acceptance

The first antidote for denial is called acceptance. Here's another way to think about it—*in order to stop our denial we must learn to develop a peaceful acceptance of the truth*. If we can calmly face the problem, acknowledge the truth about what is going on, and accept that it is happening to us, we can then develop a way for handling the situation. This peaceful acceptance shows up in our ability to stay centered and connected with our feelings while thinking about and talking about serious problems. It is the ability to calmly face and affirm the truth even if we don't like it. The person who has accepted the truth of a serious problem has the ability to honestly affirm to themselves: *"I have a serious problem! I am responsible for dealing with it! I'm willing to learn how!"*

Notice that the person may or may not be responsible for causing the problem. Addiction, like many other serious diseases and disorders, has multiple and complex causes. Some of these causes, such as our initial decision to use alcohol or drugs, were within our power to control. Another cause may be our genetic tendency to become addicted. *Whether or not you were responsible for causing the problem, you are now responsible for solving it*. You own the problem and it is yours and yours alone. You are responsible for dealing with it whether you like it or not. As a matter of fact, you have no choice but to deal with the problem. The only choice is whether you will deal with it effectively or ineffectively.

The effective management of any problem requires that you know what the problem is. In other words, you must be able to recognize and manage you own denial. You must be able to see the truth before you can take effective action. Therefore, we are all responsible for learning how to manage our own denial so we can see what is truly wrong with us and develop an effective plan for dealing with it.

Problem Solving

The second antidote for denial is problem solving. Once we recognize and accept our problems, we must learn how to solve them. Fortunately, there is a system for solving problems that we can learn how to use. Here are the six steps:

Step 1: Problem Identification: Figure out what the problem is.

Step 2: Problem Clarification: Define the problem and identify the thoughts, feelings, urges, and behaviors that you use that tend to make the problem worse.

Step 3: Identify Alternative Solutions: Think of as many possible ways to solve the problem as you can.

Step 4: Project the Logical Consequences of Each Alternative: Imagine yourself using each alternative solution and ask yourself three questions: If I try and solve the problem using this alternative solution: (1) What is the best thing that could happen? (2) What is the worst thing that could happen? And (3) What is the most likely thing that probably will happen? In other words, learn how to *think it through before you act it out*.

Step 5: Decision: Choose one of the alternative solutions that you believe will work for you. Make a decision about what you are going to do and when you are going to it.

Step 6: Action: Put your decision into action. Remember the sayings: "If nothing changes, nothing changes!" and "Easy does it, but do it."

By recognizing and accepting the problem and developing an effective problem-solving plan, our need to use denial will go down because our ability to manage our problems will go up.

Let's personalize this information by answering the following questions:

1. Can you think of a time when you were able to solve a serious problem because you were forced to look at what was really going on and deal with it? Briefly describe that experience below.

   _____
   _____
   _____
   _____
   _____
   _____
   _____
   _____
   _____

2. When you decide that something is going wrong in your life and you need to deal with it before it gets worse, what are the steps that you normally go through to figure out what is wrong and how to fix it?

   _____
   _____
   _____
   _____
   _____
   _____
   _____

3. Are you satisfied with your current ability to see what is really going wrong in your life and use effective methods to solve the problems?

   ❏ Yes ❏ No ❏ Unsure ❏ Unwilling to say

   Explain why you answered this way: _____
   _____
   _____
   _____

4. **Denial Check:** Answer the following questions to see if your denial might have been activated during this exercise

   A. Did your stress go up as you completed this exercise?

   ☐ Yes ☐ No ☐ Unsure ☐ Unwilling to say

   Explain your answer: _____

   _____

   _____

   B. Did an inner conflict or argument start in your head as you completed this exercise?

   ☐ Yes ☐ No ☐ Unsure ☐ Unwilling to say

   Explain your answer: _____

   _____

   _____

   C. Did you feel an urge to avoid answering the questions or to tell lies or half truths?

   ☐ Yes ☐ No ☐ Unsure ☐ Unwilling to say

   Explain your answer: _____

   _____

   _____

**We can learn to recognize and manage denial.
Go to the next part of this exercise to find out how.**

Exercise 2-3: Denial Can Be Recognized and Managed

We can learn to recognize and manage our denial by noticing what happens inside of us when our denial gets turned on. When denial is turned on …

- Our stress levels go up
- We get irritable and can easily get angry.
- We start to feel fearful, threatened, or unsure of ourselves for no good reason.
- We start having an inner conflict or argument in our heads.
- We start having an inner conflict. One part of us wants to avoid looking at the problem. Another part of us, wants to take a good honest look at what is really going on and set up a plan to solve the problem.

The first step in learning how to manage our denial is to learn how to sit still and notice what is going on inside of us. We need to learn how to notice what we are thinking, especially our inner conflicts and conversations, our feelings, and our urges to do things. By noticing what is going on inside of us, we can make conscious decisions about what we want to do before we blindly act out. Remember our goal: *Think it through before we act it out*.

Denial can be managed when it is recognized. Using denial is a habit. We can learn how to stop denial, look honestly at the problem, and set up a problem-solving plan. We can practice these new behaviors over and over again until they become a habit.

Not only can we learn how to manage denial. We must learn to manage it well, especially if we have a chronic, lifestyle-related disease or disorder that could destroy our lives. We can solve most problems if we recognize the truth about what is happening. Even if we can't solve a specific problem, we can learn to manage it better. An important goal of denial management is to teach people how to honestly face the truth about what is going wrong so they can learn how to manage their problems more effectively.

Let's personalize this information by answering the following questions:

1. Do you believe you sometimes use denial when it would be better for you to recognize what is really happening and set up a plan to deal with it?

   ☐ Yes ☐ No ☐ Unsure ☐ Unwilling to say

   Explain why you answered this way. _____

   _____

   _____

   _____

   _____

2. When you think that you might be using denial, what can you do to check yourself out and see if you are using denial or honestly looking at the problem?

_____
_____
_____
_____
_____

3. Once you see what the real problem is, what steps do you normally use to solve the problem?

_____
_____
_____
_____
_____

4. **Denial Check:** Answer the following questions to see if your denial might have been activated during this exercise

   A. Did your stress go up as you completed this exercise?

   ☐ Yes ☐ No ☐ Unsure ☐ Unwilling to say

   Explain your answer:_____
   _____
   _____

   B. Did an inner conflict or argument start in your head as you completed this exercise?

   ☐ Yes ☐ No ☐ Unsure ☐ Unwilling to say

   Explain your answer:_____
   _____
   _____

   C. Did you feel an urge to avoid answering the questions or tell lies or half-truths?

   ☐ Yes ☐ No ☐ Unsure ☐ Unwilling to say

   Explain your answer:_____
   _____
   _____

**To tie all of this information together into a simple definition of denial,
go to the next part of this exercise.**

Exercise 2-4: Defining Denial in a Way That Can Help Manage It

This exercise will present a definition of denial that ties together everything we have looked at it the previous exercises. Here is a simple definition of denial:

Denial is the natural tendency to avoid the pain that is caused by thinking and talking about serious problems.

By our very nature we don't like to experience pain. So when we are asked to think or talk about things that cause us to hurt, we try to avoid the pain by doing one of three things:

1. Denying that we have problems;
2. Denying that our problems are serious;
3. Denying that we are responsible for dealing with our problems.

A Real-life Experiment to See if We're in Denial

How do we know if we are in denial? How can we tell if we are seeing the truth or lying to ourselves? There is a simple experiment that will tell us if we are using denial or not. The experiment consists of writing the answers to three simple questions and noticing what happens inside of us as we are thinking about, talking about, or writing down our answers.

Here are the three things you need to pay attention to as you answer the questions that follow:

- *Does your stress go up as you answer the questions?*
- *Does an inner conflict or argument start in your head as you answer the questions. (Does one part of you start saying one thing while another part of you says something else?)*
- *Do you feel an urge to avoid answering the questions or to tell lies or half truths when you answer them.*

Pay attention to the above three things as you answer the following questions.

1. What are the three most serious problems that are going on in your life right now?

    Problem #1: _____
    _____
    _____

    Problem #2: _____
    _____
    _____

    Problem #3: _____
    _____
    _____

2. How would you rate the seriousness of those problems using a ten point scale? (10 = Very Serious, 1 = Not At All Serious)

   I rate the seriousness of my problems as: _____.

   The reason that I rate them this way: _____

   _____

   _____

3. Do you believe you are responsible for solving these problems?

   ☐ Yes ☐ No ☐ Unsure

   Explain your answer: _____

   _____

   _____

   _____

Did you write out the answers to the questions? If you did, what happened to your stress level as you answered the questions? Did you experience any inner conflicts? Did you feel an urge to avoid answering the questions or to tell lies or half truths? Did you try to avoid responsibility for the problems by blaming someone else?

If you are a normal person, you probably noticed that as you started to think about and write down your problems, your thinking and feelings changed. You may have had a hard time actually completing this simple exercise because a strong urge developed to do something else.

With the information that we learned from this simple experiment, we can define denial in a slightly different way:

Denial is a set of automatic and unconscious thoughts, feelings, and actions that protect us from the pain of thinking about and talking about our problems.

When we say that denial is *automatic*, we mean that we do it spontaneously when something happens to us. Anything that forces us to think or talk about our problems can activate or trigger denial. When we say that denial is *unconscious* we mean that we do it without thinking. When we start to think or talk about our problems, intense feelings get turned on and these feelings activate our denial. When our denial is turned on, we start to have distracting thoughts, feelings, and behaviors that shift our focus from the problem to one of the distractions. This means we have to constantly monitor ourselves or we can easily lapse into denial without even knowing it.

In order to manage our denial, we must continuously pay attention to three questions:

- *What do we start to think about that keeps us from facing our problems?*
- *What do we start to feel that keeps us from facing our problems?*
- *What do we start to do that that keeps us from facing our problems?*

We must be able to answer these three questions in order to recognize and solve our problems instead of making them worse by denying them. This means that we need to learn how to stay calm and detached while thinking and talking about our problems. This may be harder than it seems because denial is an automatic and unconscious reaction that raises our stress, scrambles our thinking, and causes us to emotionally overreact.

**Our tendency to emotionally overreact
is caused by the feelings that drive denial.
To learn about these feelings, go to the next part of this exercise.**

Exercise 2-5: The Feelings that Drive Denial

The primary feelings that drive denial are pain, anger, fear, guilt, and shame.

- We feel *pain* because we are facing difficult and seemingly overwhelming problems that are destroying our lives.

- We feel *anger* because the problems seem unfair and there is nothing we can do about them.

- We feel *fear* because we are out of control and don't know how to handle the problems.

- We feel *guilt* because, on some level, we believe that we are having these painful problems because we have done something wrong or immoral.

- We feel *shame* because we believe, on some level, that we are defective as human beings because we have these problems.

We can temporarily turn off these feelings by using denial, but these feelings almost always come back later. Later, when they come back, we use denial once again to make the feelings go away for a little while. When they come back again later we use more denial. We keep doing this over and over again until using denial becomes an automatic and unconscious habit for handling painful feelings. Because thinking and talking about serious problems almost always causes painful feelings, we actually get into the habit of using denial to manage our problems and never learn other ways to solve our problems. This means that, in many ways, *denial is the last refuge of the incompetent*. We use denial when we don't know any other way to manage our pain or solve our problems. Most of the time, we are not even consciously aware that we are using denial.

Examining the Feelings Caused by Thinking and Talking about Your Problems

1. When you think or talk about the problems that caused you to start using this workbook, do you ever feel *pain or hurt*? ☐ Yes ☐ No ☐ Unsure

   If yes, how intense is the feeling (1 = not intense; 10 = very intense) _____

   Why did you rate it this way? _____

   _____

2. When you think or talk about the problems that caused you to start using this workbook, do you ever feel *mad or angry*? ☐ Yes ☐ No ☐ Unsure

   If yes, how intense is the feeling (1 = not intense; 10 = very intense) _____

   Why did you rate it this way? _____

   _____

3. When you think or talk about the problems that caused you to start using this workbook, do you ever feel *afraid or anxious*? ☐ Yes ☐ No ☐ Unsure

   If yes, how intense is the feeling (1 = not intense; 10 = very intense) _____

   Why did you rate it this way? _____

   _____

4. When you think or talk about the problems that caused you to start using this workbook, do you ever feel *guilt or shame*? ☐ Yes ☐ No ☐ Unsure

   If yes, how intense is the feeling (1 = not intense; 10 = very intense) _____

   Why did you rate it this way? _____
   _____

5. Did you ever try to get rid of these feelings by using denial to try and convince yourself you didn't have these problems?

   ☐ Yes ☐ No ☐ Unsure Explain your answer: _____
   _____
   _____
   _____

This exercise stops here. Relax and take a break.
Your next challenge will be to learn how to recognize your own denial.

Exercise #3: Recognizing Your Denial Patterns

This exercise describes twelve common denial patterns that people tend to use to deny they have serious problems with alcohol or other drugs. You will be asked to review a denial pattern checklist that explains these denial patterns. You will then be asked to select and personalize the denial pattern you tend to use. The twelve denial patterns are:

1. **Avoidance:** "I'll talk about anything but my real problems!"

2. **Absolute Denial:** *"No not me! I don't have a problem!"*

3. **Minimizing:** "My problems aren't that bad!"

4. **Rationalizing:** "If I can find good enough reasons for my problems, I won't have to deal with them!"

5. **Blaming:** "If I can prove that my problems are not my fault, I won't have to deal with them!"

6. **Comparing:** Showing that others are worse than me proves that I don't have serious problems!"

7. **Compliance:** "I'll pretend to do what you want if you'll leave me alone!"

8. **Manipulating:** "I'll only admit that I have problems if you agree to solve them for me!"

9. **Flight into Health:** "Feeling better means that I'm cured!"

10. **Recovery by Fear:** "Being scared of my problems will make them go away!"

11. **Strategic Hopelessness:** "Because nothing works, I don't have to try!"

12. **Democratic Disease State:** "I have the right to destroy myself and no one has the right to stop me!"

Before you start reading the following list of denial patterns, take a moment to calm down, get centered, and relax. Take a deep breath. Hold it for a moment. Then slowly exhale and let yourself become deeply relaxed.

Then go on to the next page and read the description of each denial pattern out loud to yourself. Listen carefully to what the description of each denial pattern is trying to tell you. Then answer the questions that follow each denial pattern.

Go to the next page to read about Avoidance.

Exercise 3-1: Reviewing the Denial Pattern Checklist

Denial Pattern #1: Avoidance

I Say to Myself: "I'll talk about anything but my real problems!"

Somewhere deep inside of me I am afraid that I might have a problem with alcohol or drugs that is hurting me and those that I care about. But when I don't think or talk about it I feel OK. So I think about other things and try to keep people from prying into my life where they don't belong. My drinking and drugging is private and no one has a right to know anything about it. If someone asks about it, I change the subject and start talking about other things that have nothing to do with my drinking and drugging. If nothing else works, I'll start an uproar by creating a bad crisis and making sure they get sucked into it. If all else fails I'll play dumb and pretend I don't know what they're talking about.

A. As you read this denial pattern…

    (1) Did your stress go up?

        ☐ Yes ☐ No ☐ Unsure ☐ Unwilling to say

    (2) Did an inner conflict or argument start in your head?

        ☐ Yes ☐ No ☐ Unsure ☐ Unwilling to say

    (3) Did you space out, get confused, or feel an urge to stop reading?

        ☐ Yes ☐ No ☐ Unsure ☐ Unwilling to say

B. Have you ever seen other people using this denial pattern?

    ☐ Yes ☐ No ☐ Unsure ☐ Unwilling to say

If yes, describe how you saw them use this denial pattern:

_____

_____

C. Have you ever used this denial pattern?

    ☐ Yes ☐ No ☐ Unsure ☐ Unwilling to say

If yes, describe a situation when you used this denial pattern:

_____

_____

Go to the next page to learn about Absolute Denial.

Denial Pattern #2: Absolute Denial

I Say to Myself: *"No, not me! I don't have a problem!"*

When others try to corner me, I tell "the big lie." I say that I don't have a problem with alcohol or drugs. No! Not me! Absolutely not! I don't drink too much! I don't use drugs! I'm not addicted! I never get sick or have problems because of drinking or drugging. I am so good at convincing other people that there is nothing wrong that sometimes I actually start believing it myself. When they believe my story a part of me feels really good because I beat them. Another small part of me feels disappointed. There is a small part that wants others to know what is really happening. There is a small, scared part inside of me that wants help.

A. As you read this denial pattern…

    (1) Did your stress go up?

        ❏ Yes ❏ No ❏ Unsure ❏ Unwilling to say

    (2) Did an inner conflict or argument start in your head?

        ❏ Yes ❏ No ❏ Unsure ❏ Unwilling to say

    (3) Did you space out, get confused, or feel an urge to stop reading?

        ❏ Yes ❏ No ❏ Unsure ❏ Unwilling to say

B. Have you ever seen other people using this denial pattern?

    ❏ Yes ❏ No ❏ Unsure ❏ Unwilling to say

    If yes, describe how you saw them use this denial pattern:

    _____
    _____
    _____

C. Have you ever used this denial pattern?

    ❏ Yes ❏ No ❏ Unsure ❏ Unwilling to say

    If yes, describe a situation when you used this denial pattern:

    _____
    _____
    _____

Go to the next page to learn about Minimizing.

Denial Pattern #3: Minimizing

I Say to Myself: *"My problems aren't that bad!"*

Sometimes my alcohol and drug problems get so bad I can't convince myself or others that I don't have a problem. When this happens I minimize. I make the problems seem smaller than they really are. Yes, I had a small problem with my drinking and drugging. But it only happened that once. It will never happen again. Besides, the problem just wasn't as bad as people think it is.

A. As you read this denial pattern...

    (1) Did your stress go up?

        ☐ Yes ☐ No ☐ Unsure ☐ Unwilling to say

    (2) Did an inner conflict or argument start in your head?

        ☐ Yes ☐ No ☐ Unsure ☐ Unwilling to say

    (3) Did you space out, get confused, or feel an urge to stop reading?

        ☐ Yes ☐ No ☐ Unsure ☐ Unwilling to say

B. Have you ever *seen other people* using this denial pattern?

    ☐ Yes ☐ No ☐ Unsure ☐ Unwilling to say

    If yes, describe how you saw them use this denial pattern:

    _____

    _____

    _____

C. Have you ever used this denial pattern?

    ☐ Yes ☐ No ☐ Unsure ☐ Unwilling to say

    If yes, describe a situation when you used this denial pattern:

    _____

    _____

    _____

Go to the next page to read about Rationalizing.

Denial Pattern #4: Rationalizing

I Say to Myself: *"If I can find good enough reasons for my problems, I won't have to deal with them!"*

I try to explain away my alcohol and drug problems by making up good explanations for why I drink and what's "really" causing my problems. Sometimes I'll pretend to know a lot about alcoholism and addiction so other people will think that I know too much to have a problem. The truth is that I rarely, if ever, apply what I know to myself or to my own problems.

A. As you read this denial pattern…

    (1) Did your stress go up?

        ❒ Yes ❒ No ❒ Unsure ❒ Unwilling to say

    (2) Did an inner conflict or argument start in your head?

        ❒ Yes ❒ No ❒ Unsure ❒ Unwilling to say

    (3) Did you space out, get confused, or feel an urge to stop reading?

        ❒ Yes ❒ No ❒ Unsure ❒ Unwilling to say

B. Have you ever *seen other people* using this denial pattern?

    ❒ Yes ❒ No ❒ Unsure ❒ Unwilling to say

If yes, describe how you saw them use this denial pattern:

_____

_____

_____

C. Have you ever used this denial pattern?

    ❒ Yes ❒ No ❒ Unsure ❒ Unwilling to say

If yes, describe a situation when you used this denial pattern:

_____

_____

_____

Go to the next page to read about Blaming.

Denial Pattern #5: Blaming

I Say to Myself: *"If I can prove that my problems are not my fault, I won't have to deal with them!"*

When the problems get so bad that I can't deny it, I find a scapegoat. I tell everyone that it's not my fault that I have these problems with alcohol and drugs. It's somebody else's fault. I only abuse alcohol and drugs because of my partner. If you were with a person like this, you'd abuse alcohol and drugs too! If you had a job or a boss like mine, you'd drink and drug as much as I do. It seems that as long as I can blame someone else, I can keep drinking and drugging until that person changes. I don't have to be responsible for stopping.

A. As you read this denial pattern…

(1) Did your stress go up?
☐ Yes ☐ No ☐ Unsure ☐ Unwilling to say

(2) Did an inner conflict or argument start in your head?
☐ Yes ☐ No ☐ Unsure ☐ Unwilling to say

(3) Did you space out, get confused, or feel an urge to stop reading?
☐ Yes ☐ No ☐ Unsure ☐ Unwilling to say

B. Have you ever *seen other people* using this denial pattern?
☐ Yes ☐ No ☐ Unsure ☐ Unwilling to say

If yes, describe how you saw them use this denial pattern:

_____
_____
_____

C. Have you ever used this denial pattern?
☐ Yes ☐ No ☐ Unsure ☐ Unwilling to say

If yes, describe a situation when you used this denial pattern:

_____
_____
_____

Go to the next page to read about Comparing.

Denial Pattern #6: Comparing

I Say to Myself: *"Showing that others are worse than me proves that I don't have serious problems!"*

I start to focus on other people instead of myself. I find others who have more serious alcohol and drug problems than I do and compare myself to them. I tell myself that I can't be addicted because I'm not as bad as they are. I know what an addict is! An addict is someone who drinks and drugs a lot more than I do! An addict is someone who has a lot more alcohol and drug-related problems than I do. An addict is someone who is not like me! I tell myself that I can't be addicted because there are other people who have worse problems with alcohol and drugs than I do.

A. As you read this denial pattern…

    (1) Did your stress go up?

        ☐ Yes ☐ No ☐ Unsure ☐ Unwilling to say

    (2) Did an inner conflict or argument start in your head?

        ☐ Yes ☐ No ☐ Unsure ☐ Unwilling to say

    (3) Did you space out, get confused, or feel an urge to stop reading?

        ☐ Yes ☐ No ☐ Unsure ☐ Unwilling to say

B. Have you ever *seen other people* using this denial pattern?

    ☐ Yes ☐ No ☐ Unsure ☐ Unwilling to say

If yes, describe how you saw them use this denial pattern:

_____
_____
_____

C. Have you ever used this denial pattern?

    ☐ Yes ☐ No ☐ Unsure ☐ Unwilling to say

If yes, describe a situation when you used this denial pattern:

_____
_____
_____

Go to the next page to read about Compliance.

Denial Pattern #7: Compliance

I Say to Myself: *"I'll pretend to do what you want if you'll leave me alone!"*

I start going through the motions of getting help. I do what I'm told, no more and no less. I become compliant and promise to do things just to get people off my back. I find excuses for not following through. When I get caught, I tell people that I did the best I could. I blame them for not giving me enough help. I tell people how sorry I am. I ask for another chance, make another half-hearted commitment, and the cycle of compliance starts all over again.

A. As you read this denial pattern…

    (1) Did your stress go up?

        ☐ Yes ☐ No ☐ Unsure ☐ Unwilling to say

    (2) Did an inner conflict or argument start in your head?

        ☐ Yes ☐ No ☐ Unsure ☐ Unwilling to say

    (3) Did you space out, get confused, or feel an urge to stop reading?

        ☐ Yes ☐ No ☐ Unsure ☐ Unwilling to say

B. Have you ever *seen other people* using this denial pattern?

    ☐ Yes ☐ No ☐ Unsure ☐ Unwilling to say

If yes, describe how you saw them use this denial pattern:

_____
_____
_____

C. Have you ever used this denial pattern?

    ☐ Yes ☐ No ☐ Unsure ☐ Unwilling to say

If yes, describe a situation when you used this denial pattern:

_____
_____
_____

Go to the next page to read about Manipulating.

Denial Pattern #8: Manipulating

I Say to Myself: *"I'll only admit that I have problems if you agree to solve them for me!"*

When my alcohol and drug problems box me into a corner, I start to manipulate. I try to use the people who want to help me. I try to get them to handle all of my problems and then get them to leave me alone so I can keep drinking and drugging. I'll let them help me, but only if they do it for me. I want a quick effortless fix. If they can't fix me, I blame them for my failure and use them as an excuse to keep drinking and drugging. I won't let anyone make me do anything that I don't want to do. If they try, I'll get angry at them, blame them, and make them feel guilty.

A. As you read this denial pattern...

   (1) Did your stress go up?

   ☐ Yes ☐ No ☐ Unsure ☐ Unwilling to say

   (2) Did an inner conflict or argument start in your head?

   ☐ Yes ☐ No ☐ Unsure ☐ Unwilling to say

   (3) Did you space out, get confused, or feel an urge to stop reading?

   ☐ Yes ☐ No ☐ Unsure ☐ Unwilling to say

B. Have you ever *seen other people* using this denial pattern?

   ☐ Yes ☐ No ☐ Unsure ☐ Unwilling to say

   If yes, describe how you saw them use this denial pattern:

   _____
   _____
   _____

C. Have you ever used this denial pattern?

   ☐ Yes ☐ No ☐ Unsure ☐ Unwilling to say

   If yes, describe a situation when you used this denial pattern:

   _____
   _____
   _____

Go to the next page to read about Flight into Health.

Denial Pattern #9: Flight into Health

I Say to Myself: *"Feeling better means that I'm cured!"*

I manage to stay clean and sober for a while, and things start to get a little bit better. Instead of getting motivated to do more, I convince myself that I'm cured and don't need to do anything. I tell myself that I may have had a drinking and drug problem, but I got into recovery and put it behind me.

A. As you read this denial pattern…

(1) Did your stress go up?
☐ Yes ☐ No ☐ Unsure ☐ Unwilling to say

(2) Did an inner conflict or argument start in your head?
☐ Yes ☐ No ☐ Unsure ☐ Unwilling to say

(3) Did you space out, get confused, or feel an urge to stop reading?
☐ Yes ☐ No ☐ Unsure ☐ Unwilling to say

B. Have you ever *seen other people* using this denial pattern?
☐ Yes ☐ No ☐ Unsure ☐ Unwilling to say

If yes, describe how you saw them use this denial pattern:

_____
_____
_____

C. Have you ever used this denial pattern?
☐ Yes ☐ No ☐ Unsure ☐ Unwilling to say

If yes, describe a situation when you used this denial pattern:

_____
_____
_____

Go to the next page to read about Recovery by Fear.

Denial Pattern #10: Recovery by Fear

I Say to Myself: *"Being scared of my problems will make them go away!"*

I began to realize that alcohol and other drugs can destroy my life, hurt those I love, and eventually kill me. The threat is so real that I convince myself I can't ever use alcohol or drugs again. I start to believe that this fear of destroying my life and killing myself will scare me into permanent sobriety. Since I now know how awful my life will be if I continue to drink and drug, I just won't drink or drug anymore. If I just stop, everything will be fine, and I won't need treatment or a recovery program. I'll just quit.

A. As you read this denial pattern…

    (1) Did your stress go up?

        ☐ Yes ☐ No ☐ Unsure ☐ Unwilling to say

    (2) Did an inner conflict or argument start in your head?

        ☐ Yes ☐ No ☐ Unsure ☐ Unwilling to say

    (3) Did you space out, get confused, or feel an urge to stop reading?

        ☐ Yes ☐ No ☐ Unsure ☐ Unwilling to say

B. Have you ever *seen other people* using this denial pattern?

    ☐ Yes ☐ No ☐ Unsure ☐ Unwilling to say

If yes, describe how you saw them use this denial pattern:

_____

_____

_____

C. Have you ever used this denial pattern?

    ☐ Yes ☐ No ☐ Unsure ☐ Unwilling to say

If yes, describe a situation when you used this denial pattern:

_____

_____

_____

Go to the next page to read about Strategic Hopelessness.

Denial Pattern #11: Strategic Hopelessness

I Say to Myself: *"Since nothing works, I don't have to try"*

I start to feel that I'm hopeless. It seems like I've done it all and nothing works. I don't believe I can change and a big part of me just doesn't want to try anymore. It seems easier just to give up. When people try to help me, I brush them off by telling them that I'm hopeless and will never recover. When people do try to help me, I give them a hard time and make it impossible for them to help me. I don't understand why people want to help me. It would be easier if they just let me keep drinking and drugging.

A. As you read this denial pattern…

    (1) Did your stress go up?

        ☐ Yes ☐ No ☐ Unsure ☐ Unwilling to say

    (2) Did an inner conflict or argument start in your head?

        ☐ Yes ☐ No ☐ Unsure ☐ Unwilling to say

    (3) Did you space out, get confused, or feel an urge to stop reading?

        ☐ Yes ☐ No ☐ Unsure ☐ Unwilling to say

B. Have you ever *seen other people* using this denial pattern?

    ☐ Yes ☐ No ☐ Unsure ☐ Unwilling to say

    If yes, describe how you saw them use this denial pattern:

    _____

    _____

    _____

C. Have you ever used this denial pattern?

    ☐ Yes ☐ No ☐ Unsure ☐ Unwilling to say

    If yes, describe a situation when you used this denial pattern:

    _____

    _____

    _____

Go to the next page to read about the Democratic Disease State.

Denial Pattern #12: The Democratic Disease State

I Say to Myself: *"I have the right to destroy myself and no one has the right to stop me!"*

I convince myself that I have a right to continue to use alcohol and drugs even if it kills me. Yes, I'm addicted. Yes I'm destroying my life. Yes, I'm hurting those I love. Yes, I'm a burden to society. So what? I have the right to drink and drug myself to death. No one has the right to make me stop. My addiction is killing me anyway, I might as well convince myself that I'm dying because I want to.

A. As you read this denial pattern…

    (1) Did your stress go up?

        ☐ Yes ☐ No ☐ Unsure ☐ Unwilling to say

    (2) Did an inner conflict or argument start in your head?

        ☐ Yes ☐ No ☐ Unsure ☐ Unwilling to say

    (3) Did you space out, get confused, or feel an urge to stop reading?

        ☐ Yes ☐ No ☐ Unsure ☐ Unwilling to say

B. Have you ever *seen other people* using this denial pattern?

    ☐ Yes ☐ No ☐ Unsure ☐ Unwilling to say

    If yes, describe how you saw them use this denial pattern:

    _____

    _____

    _____

C. Have you ever used this denial pattern?

    ☐ Yes ☐ No ☐ Unsure ☐ Unwilling to say

    If yes, describe a situation when you used this denial pattern:

    _____

    _____

    _____

Take a short break. Then go to the next part of the exercise to learn how to write Personalized Denial Patterns.

Exercise 3-2: Learning How to Personalize Denial Patterns

In order for us to learn how to recognize and manage our own denial, we need to learn how to personalize the denial patterns that we selected. We personalize denial patterns by writing a new title and description for each one in our own words. For example, I could rewrite the title for *Avoidance* as *"Beating around the Bush"* or *"Skating Off the Walls."*

The next step is to write a description of the denial pattern that begins with the words: "I know that I'm using denial when I...." Notice the word "I" at the end of this phrase. This means that the person who is personalizing the denial pattern should always be the subject of the sentence.

Here are some examples of personalized denial patterns. These examples are meant to show you how I would personalize each denial pattern. The examples are written in my words not yours. If you just copy my words you are not personalizing the denial patterns. For this exercise to work for you, you will need to use whatever time and energy it takes to write the titles and descriptions in your own words that really mean something to you and that will be easy to remember.

This workbook only asks you to personalize three denial patterns. I've given examples of all twelve to make sure you have an example of the three that you selected.

1. (Avoidance) **Skating Off the Walls:** I know I'm using denial when I refuse to directly answer a question and keep trying to change the subject.

2. (Absolute Denial) **It Isn't So:** I know I'm using denial when I tell people that I don't have a problem even though I know deep inside that I do.

3. (Minimizing) **It Isn't That Bad:** I know I'm using denial when I admit that I have a problem, but try to tell people that it isn't as bad as they think it is.

4. (Rationalizing) **Giving Good Reasons:** I know I'm using denial when I try to convince people that there are good reasons for me to have the problem and that because there are good reasons I shouldn't be responsible for having to deal with it.

5. (Blaming) **It's Not My Fault:** I know I'm using denial when I try to blame someone else for my problem and deny that I am responsible for dealing with it.

6. (Comparison) **Criticizing Others:** I know I'm using denial when I point out how bad other people's problems are and use that as a reason why my problems aren't so bad.

7. (Manipulating) **Getting Over On Others:** I know I'm using denial when I try to get other people to handle the problems for me.

8. (Recovery by Fear) **Scared Straight:** I know I'm using denial when I tell myself that I could never use alcohol or drugs again because I'm so afraid of what will happen if I start drinking and drugging.

9. (Compliance) **Being a Good Little Boy:** I know I'm using denial when I start telling people what they want to hear to get them off my back.

10. (Flight into Health) **Suddenly Cured:** I know I'm using denial when I believe my problems have suddenly gone away without my doing anything to solve them.

11. (Strategic Hopelessness) **Why Bother?:** I know I'm using denial when I tell myself that I can never solve my problems and that other people should just leave me alone.

12. (Democratic Disease State) **I Have My Rights:** I know I'm using denial when I tell other people that I have a right to use alcohol and drugs regardless of what happens and that they have no right to try and stop me.

Take a short break. Then go to the next part of the exercise to identify the three denial patterns you used most frequently in the past. *Remember—copying the examples above won't be very helpful.*

Exercise 3-3: Selecting the Denial Patterns You Tend to Use

Review the *Denial Pattern Checklist* and select three denial patterns you have used in the past. Write the title of the three denial patterns below. Be sure to copy the title directly from the *Denial Pattern Checklist.* Put the denial pattern you tend to use most frequently first.

A. Denial Pattern #1: _____

B. Denial Pattern #2: _____

C. Denial Pattern #3: _____

**Go to the next part of the exercise
to learn how to personalize the denial pattern you selected.**

Exercise 3-4: Personalizing the First Denial Pattern You Selected

Instructions: Answer the following questions about the first denial pattern you selected. Keep your answers short and to the point.

1. What is the first denial pattern you selected? Be sure to copy the title from *Exercise 3-3*.

   _____

2. Why did you select this denial pattern?

   _____
   _____

3. Go back to the *Denial Pattern Checklist* and read the description of the denial pattern again. Underline what you consider the most important word or phrase. What word or phrase did you underline? Write it below.

   _____

4. What does this word or phrase mean to you?

   _____
   _____

5. Write a *personal title* for this denial pattern that will be easy for you to remember. The title should be no longer than two or three words.

   _____

6. Write a *personal description* for this denial pattern. Make sure the description is a single sentence that begins with the words, *I know I'm going into denial when I start to....* Don't use any of the words from your personal title (question 5 above) in this personal description.

   I know I'm going into denial when I start to… _____
   _____
   _____
   _____

**Go to the next page and answer the questions for
the second denial pattern you selected.**

Exercise 3-5: Personalizing the Second Denial Pattern You Selected

Instructions: Answer the following questions about the second denial pattern you selected. Keep your answers short and to the point.

1. What is the second denial pattern you selected? Be sure to copy the title from *Exercise 3-3*.

   _____

2. Why did you select this denial pattern?

   _____
   _____

3. Go back to the *Denial Pattern Checklist* and read the description of the denial pattern again. Underline what you consider the most important word or phrase. What word or phrase did you underline? Write it below.

   _____

4. What does this word or phrase mean to you?

   _____
   _____

5. Write a *personal title* for this denial pattern that will be easy for you to remember. The title should be no longer than two or three words.

   _____

6. Write a *personal description* for this denial pattern. Make sure the description is a single sentence that begins with the words, *I know I'm going into denial when I start to…*. Don't use any of the words from your personal title (question 5 above) in this personal description.

   I know I'm going into denial when I start to… _____
   _____
   _____
   _____

Go to the next page and answer the questions for the third denial pattern you selected.

Exercise 3-6: Personalizing the Third Denial Pattern You Selected

Instructions: Answer the following questions about the third denial pattern you selected. Keep your answers short and to the point.

1. What is the third denial pattern you selected? Be sure to copy the title from *Exercise 3-3*.

   _____

2. Why did you select this denial pattern?

   _____
   _____

3. Go back to the *Denial Pattern Checklist* and read the description of the denial pattern again. Underline what you consider the most important word or phrase. What word or phrase did you underline? Write it below.

   _____

4. What does this word or phrase mean to you?

   _____
   _____

5. Write a *personal title* for this denial pattern that will be easy for you to remember. The title should be no longer than two or three words.

   _____

6. Write a *personal description* for this denial pattern. Make sure the description is a single sentence that begins with the words, *I know I'm going into denial when I start to...*. Don't use any of the words from your personal title (question 5 above) in this personal description.

   I know I'm going into denial when I start to... _____
   _____
   _____
   _____

This exercise ends here. Relax and take a break

Exercise #4: Managing Denial

In this exercise you will learn how to manage the three denial patterns you selected and personalized in the last exercise. If you notice that you begin to use other denial patterns, you can also use the same methods to learn how to manage them.

Using denial patterns activates deeply entrenched habits of thinking, feeling, acting, and relating to others that make it difficult for us to identify and solve our problems. To effectively manage these denial patterns, *we must learn to recognize and stop denial quickly when it occurs*. Our chances of doing this get better as we learn how to recognize and manage the thoughts, feelings, urges, actions, and social reactions that are associated with each denial pattern.

In order to recognize and stop denial quickly when it occurs, we need to learn how to stop our automatic unconscious reactions to the denial, and learn how to pause and respond with conscious choices instead.

Unconscious Reactions are automatic habitual things that we do when something happens. There are four things that we automatically do when something happens to us: think about it, have feelings about it, get an urge to do something about it, or actually do something about it. We normally don't pay attention to these different parts of the reaction. A trigger goes off, we react, something happens because of what we did and we start reacting to the new problems we created by our first reactions.

To learn how to manage denial we have to learn how to recognize the different ways that we respond to the denial once it is activated. Our reactions to denial can be broken down into its component parts which are: (1) automatic thoughts, (2) automatic feelings, (3) automatic urges, and (4) automatic actions. To learn how to effectively deal with our denial, we must learn how to turn automatic reactions into conscious choices.

Conscious Choices are different from unconscious reactions. An unconscious reaction is automatic, we do it without thinking. A conscious choice is something we make a decision to do. In order to manage our denial, we must learn to make better choices about how we consciously respond to our denial. In other words, we need to consciously choose what we think, how we manage and express our feelings, how we manage our urges, and what we actually do when our denial is activated. By doing this we can learn how to quickly turn off the denial and get focused upon identifying and solving the painful problem that activated the denial.

In this exercise on *managing our denial patterns*, we will learn how to identify the thoughts, feelings, urges, actions, and social reactions associated with the three denial patterns that you selected and personalized in *Exercise 3*. Then we will learn how to turn off each denial pattern by changing what we are thinking, how we are managing our feelings and urges, what we are doing, and how we are relating to other people.

The first thing that we need to do is to understand how thoughts, feelings, urges, actions, and social reactions relate to one another. Here are some basic principles that can help us understand how this works.

1. *Thoughts Cause Feelings*. Whenever we think about something we automatically react by having a feeling or an emotion.

2. *Thoughts And Feelings Work Together to Cause Urges.* Our way of thinking causes us to feel certain things. These feelings, in turn, reinforce the way we are thinking. These thoughts and feelings work together to create an urge to do something. An urge is a desire that may be rational or irrational. The irrational urge to use alcohol or other drugs, even though we know that it will hurt us is also called *craving*. It is irrational because we want to use alcohol or other drugs even though we know it will not be good for us.

3. *Urges Plus Decisions Cause Actions.* When we feel an urge we can pause and decide to do something about it or to do nothing. This pause between the urge and action is called *a decision point*. Decision points are critically important because what we do or don't do at a decision point will determine what happens next.

   A decision is a choice. A choice is a specific way of thinking that causes us to commit to one way of doing things while refusing to do anything else. The decision point is the space between the urge and the action and it is always filled with a decision. The decision may be an automatic and unconscious choice that we have learned to make without having to think about it, or the decision can be based upon a conscious choice that results from carefully reflecting upon the situation and the options available for dealing with it.

4. *Actions Cause Reactions from Other People.* Our actions affect other people and cause them to react to us. It is helpful to think about our behavior like invitations that we give to other people to treat us in certain ways. Some behaviors invite people to be nice to us and to treat us with respect. Other behaviors invite people to argue and fight with us or to put us down. In every social situation we share part of the responsibility for what happens. This is because we are constantly inviting people to respond to us by the actions we take and by how we react to what other people do.

To recognize and stop our denial we need to learn how to: (1) tell the difference between thoughts and feelings; (2) tell the difference between feelings and urges; (3) tell the difference between urges and actions; (4) tell the difference between our actions and the social reaction they cause.

Learning how to manage our denial patterns, teaches us *how to control our impulses*. We don't have to do whatever we feel an urge to do. We can learn to stop our automatic reactions and start to make conscious choices. We can do this by learning how to *pause, relax, reflect, and decide*. We can learn to control our impulses even when we feel a strong urge to do something immediately. It's not easy, but we can learn how. Let's look at these four steps of the impulse control process:

- *Pause* and notice the urge without doing anything about it;
- *Relax* by taking a deep breath, slowly exhaling, and consciously imagining the stress draining from your body;
- *Reflect* on what you are experiencing by asking yourself: "What do I have an urge to do? What has happened when I have done similar things in the past? What is likely to happen if I do that now?" Then,
- *Decide* what you are going to do about the urge. Make a conscious choice instead of acting out in an automatic an unconscious way. When making the choice about

what you are going to do, remind yourself that you will be responsible for both the action and its consequences.

Remember: *Impulse control lives in the space between the urge and the action.*

With this in mind, let's review the basic principles for managing denial that are used in this exercise:

1. Writing a *Personal Title* for each denial pattern makes it easier for us to remember the denial pattern and call it to mind when we need to.

2. Writing a *Personal Description* for each denial pattern makes it easier for us to clearly understand what the denial pattern is, and to explain it to other people so they can tell us when they see us using it.

3. Identifying the *irrational thoughts* that are associated with each denial pattern makes it easier for us to develop new ways of thinking that will stop denial and help us start identifying and solving our problems.

4. Identifying the *unmanageable feelings* associated with each denial pattern makes it easier to develop new ways of managing those feelings.

5. Identifying the *self-destructive urges* that are associated with each denial pattern makes it easier for us to recognize the urge before we act it out, and consciously choose to do something different.

6. Identifying the *self-defeating actions* associated with each denial pattern makes it easier for us to develop new ways of acting.

7. Identifying the reactions of others that support each denial pattern makes it easier to develop new ways of inviting people to help us stop using denial and start identifying and solving our problems.

**Go to the next page and explore
how to manage the first denial pattern you selected.**

Exercise 4-1: Managing the First Denial Pattern You Selected

1. Write the *Personal Title* of the first denial pattern you selected.

   _____

2. Write the *Personal Description* of the first denial pattern you selected.

   _____

   _____

3. When you're using this denial pattern, what do you tend to think?	What is another way ot thinking that will allow you to stop denial and start identifying and solving your problem?
_____ _____ _____ _____ _____	_____ _____ _____ _____ _____
4. When you're using this denial pattern, what do you tend to feel?	How could you manage those feelings in a way that will allow you to stop denial and start identifying and solving your problems?
_____ _____ _____ _____ _____	_____ _____ _____ _____ _____
5. When you're using this denial pattern, what do you have an urge to do?	How could you manage the urge by doing something that will help you stop denial and start identifying and solving your problems?
_____ _____ _____ _____ _____	_____ _____ _____ _____ _____

6. When you're using this denial pattern, what do you usually do?	What else could you do that would help you stop denial and start identifying and solving your problems?
_____ _____ _____ _____ _____	_____ _____ _____ _____ _____
7. When you're using this denial pattern, how do other people usually react?	How could you invite people to react to you in a way that would help you stop denial and start identifying and solving your problems?
_____ _____ _____ _____ _____	_____ _____ _____ _____ _____

**Go to the next page and explore
how to manage the second denial pattern you selected.**

Exercise 4-2: Managing the Second Denial Pattern You Selected

1. Write the *Personal Title* of the second denial pattern you selected.

   _____

2. Write the *Personal Description* of the second denial pattern you selected.

   _____

   _____

3. When you're using this denial pattern, what do you tend to think?	What is another way ot thinking that will allow you to stop denial and start identifying and solving your problem?
_____ _____ _____ _____ _____ _____	_____ _____ _____ _____ _____ _____
4. When you're using this denial pattern, what do you tend to feel?	How could you manage those feelings in a way that will allow you to stop denial and start identifying and solving your problems?
_____ _____ _____ _____ _____ _____	_____ _____ _____ _____ _____ _____
5. When you're using this denial pattern, what do you have an urge to do?	How could you manage the urge by doing something that will help you stop denial and start identifying and solving your problems?
_____ _____ _____ _____ _____ _____	_____ _____ _____ _____ _____ _____

6. When you're using this denial pattern, what do you usually do?	What else could you do that would help you stop denial and start identifying and solving your problems?
_____ _____ _____ _____ _____ _____	_____ _____ _____ _____ _____ _____
7. When you're using this denial pattern, how do other people usually react?	How could you invite people to react to you in a way that would help you stop denial and start identifying and solving your problems?
_____ _____ _____ _____ _____ _____	_____ _____ _____ _____ _____ _____

**Go to the next page and explore
how to manage the third denial pattern you selected.**

Exercise 4-3: Managing the Third Denial Pattern You Selected

1. Write the *Personal Title* of the third denial pattern you selected.

   _____

2. Write the *Personal Description* of the third denial pattern you selected.

   _____
   _____

3. When you're using this denial pattern, what do you tend to think?	What is another way ot thinking that will allow you to stop denial and start identifying and solving your problem?
_____ _____ _____ _____ _____	_____ _____ _____ _____ _____
4. When you're using this denial pattern, what do you tend to feel?	How could you manage those feelings in a way that will allow you to stop denial and start identifying and solving your problems?
_____ _____ _____ _____ _____	_____ _____ _____ _____ _____
5. When you're using this denial pattern, what do you have an urge to do?	How could you manage the urge by doing something that will help you stop denial and start identifying and solving your problems?
_____ _____ _____ _____ _____	_____ _____ _____ _____ _____

6. When you're using this denial pattern, what do you usually do?	What else could you do that would help you stop denial and start identifying and solving your problems?
_____ _____ _____ _____ _____	_____ _____ _____ _____ _____
7. When you're using this denial pattern, how do other people usually react?	How could you invite people to react to you in a way that would help you stop denial and start identifying and solving your problems?
_____ _____ _____ _____ _____	_____ _____ _____ _____ _____

Go to the next page and bring together everything you learned about managing denial from the last three parts of this exercise.

Exercise 4-4: Bringing Your Denial Management Skills Together

1. Review your answers to question 3 on *Exercises 4-1, 4-2,* and *4-3*. In the first column below make a combined list of all the thoughts associated with the three denial patterns that you selected. In the second column below make a combined list of all the new ways of thinking that could help you stop denial.

The thoughts associated with my three denial patterns are…	The new ways of thinking that could stop my denial are…

2. Review your answers to question 4 on *Exercises 4-1, 4-2,* and *4-3*. In the first column below make a combined list of all the feelings that are associated with the three denial patterns that you selected. In the second column below make a combined list of all of new feeling management strategies that could help you stop denial.

The feelings associated with my three denial patterns are…	The new ways of managing those feelings that could stop my denial are…

3. Review your answers to question 5 on *Exercises 4-1, 4-2,* and *4-3*. In the first column below make a combined list of all the urges that are associated with the three denial patterns you selected. In the second column below make a combined list of all the new ways of managing those urges that could help you stop denial.

The urges associated with my three denial patterns are…	The new ways of managing those urges that could stop my denial are…

4. Review your answers to question 6 on *Exercises 4-1, 4-2,* and *4-3*. In the first column below make a combined list of all the self-defeating actions (self-defeating behaviors) that are associated with the three denial patterns you selected. In the second column below make a combined list of all the new ways of behaving that could help you stop denial.

The behaviors associated with my three denial patterns are…	The new behaviors that could stop my denial are…

5. Review your answers to question 7 on *Exercises 4-1, 4-2,* and *4-3*. In the first column below make a combined list of all the self-defeating actions (self-defeating behaviors) that are associated with the three denial patterns you selected. In the second column below make a combined list of all the new ways of behaving that could help you stop denial.

The ways I invite others to become part of my three denial patterns are…	The new ways I could invite others to help me stop my denial are…

6. After reviewing all of the information that you organized above, what are the three most important things you could do that would help you stop using denial and start identifying and solving your problems?

   A. The most important thing I could do to stop my denial is…

   B. The second most important thing I could do to stop my denial is…

   C. The third most important thing I could do to stop my denial is…

**This exercise ends here. Take a break and get ready for a real challenge:
Stopping denial as you think and talk about your problems.**

Exercise #5: Stopping Denial as You Think about Your Problems

In this exercise we will start applying our new denial management skills to our problems. This isn't easy because we will be asked to think and talk about serious and painful problems. Even though most of us start this exercise intending to be honest, we find that our denial gets activated. Whenever we become aware that we are using denial, we can turn it of by pausing, relaxing, reflecting, and deciding. We *pause* and notice that we are using denial. We don't do anything about it. Then we *relax* by taking a deep breath, slowly exhaling, and consciously imagining the stress drain from our body. Next we *reflect* on what we are experiencing by asking ourselves: "Do I really want to keep using denial, or do I want to look at what is really going on so I can decide what I want to do about it?" Finally we *decide* whether or not we will keep using denial. When making this choice, remind yourself that you will be responsible for the consequences.

This exercise has four parts. In *Exercise 5-1* we examine the presenting problems that caused us to seek help at this time. While answering the questions we will ask you to carefully monitor yourself for denial. At first this will probably be difficult. Many of us don't even notice that we used denial until after we complete the exercise and read our answers.

In *Exercise 5-2* we examine the relationship between each of our presenting problems and our use of alcohol or other drugs. Once again we use self-monitoring to recognize and stop our denial. Most of us find it getting a little easier to recognize and stop your denial than it was in the first part.

In *Exercise 5-3* we examine what will probably happen to each problem if we keep using alcohol or other drugs. Once again we monitor ourselves for denial and stop it whenever possible. Most of us find the process getting a little easier.

In *Exercise 5-4* we summarize all of the information from the first three exercises on a single worksheet and make some hard decisions about what we are going to do about our alcohol and drug use. Once again we monitor our denial and recognize it and stop it when we can. By this time most of us are getting into the habit of using denial management, so the process gets even easier than before.

The self-monitoring section of each part of this exercise consists of reviewing a checklist of denial patterns to see which, if any, we used during the exercise. At first, most of us don't notice that we were using denial until after we have complete an exercise and read our answers. Seeing that we used denial without even knowing it can make us feel pretty dumb. But remember, denial is an automatic and unconscious process. It takes a lot of hard work to learn how to recognize and stop it. Besides, look on the bright side: Before this, you never even knew for sure when you were using denial and when you weren't. So, you've made progress.

Once we learn to recognize denial as we are using it, we have a chance to practice stopping it. Finally we learn to recognize the urge to use denial which gives us the power to choose to look at the truth without ever using denial.

Exercise 5-1: The Problems that Caused You to Seek Help

What are the three most important problems that caused you to seek help at this time? A *problem title* is a word or a short phrase that is easy to remember. A *problem description* is a sentence or short paragraph that describes what the problem is.

1. **Title for Problem #1:** _____

   Description: The first problem that caused me to start using this workbook:

   _____

   _____

   How serious is the problem? (0 = not at all serious; 10 = very serious): _____

2. **Title for Problem #2:** _____

   Description: The second problem that caused me to start using this workbook:

   _____

   _____

   How serious is the problem? (0 = not at all serious; 10 = very serious): _____

3. **Title for Problem #3:** _____

   Description: The third problem that caused me to start using this workbook:

   _____

   _____

   How serious is the problem? (0 = not at all serious; 10 = very serious): _____

4. **Denial Check:** Complete the two-part denial check below.

Part 1: What denial patterns did you use during this part of the exercise? (Check as many as needed.)	
1. **Avoidance:** "I'll talk about anything but my real problems."	7. **Compliance:** "I'll pretend to do what you want if you'll leave me alone."
2. **Absolute Denial:** "No not Me, I don't have problems."	8. **Manipulating:** "I'll only admit that I have problems if you agree to solve them for me."
3. **Minimizing:** "My problems aren't that bad."	9. **Flight Into Health:** "Feeling better means that I'm cured."
4. **Rationalizing:** "If I can find good enough reasons for my problems, I won't have to deal with them."	10. **Recovery by Fear:** "Being scared of my problems will make them go away."
5. **Blaming:** "If I can prove that my problems are not my fault, I won't have to deal with them."	11. **Strategic Hopelessness:** "Since nothing works, I don't have to try."
6. **Comparing:** "Showing that others are worse than me proves that I don't have serious problems."	12. **Democratic Disease State:** "I have the right to destroy myself and no one has the right to stop me."

Part 2: When did you notice you were using denial?
A. Not until after completing this part of the exercise and reading my answers.
B. While I was answering the questions.
C. I noticed the urge to start using denial before I started to answer the question, but I ended up using denial when I answered the questions anyway.
D. I noticed the urge to start using denial before I started to answer the question, and stopped my denial and answered the questions honestly.

Exercise 5-2: The Relationship of Your Problems to Alcohol and Drug Use

1. Write Your Title for Problem #1: _____

   What is the relationship between Problem #1 and your use of alcohol or other drugs?

   A. Did using alcohol or other drugs cause this problem? (Would you have this problem if you never used alcohol or other drugs?)

   ☐ Yes ☐ No ☐ Unsure ☐ Unwilling to say

   Explain why you answered this way? _____
   _____
   _____

   B. Did using alcohol or other drugs make this problem worse than it would have been if you hadn't been using?

   ☐ Yes ☐ No ☐ Unsure ☐ Unwilling to say

   Explain why you answered this way? _____
   _____
   _____

   C. Did you use alcohol or other drugs to deal with stress or pain caused by this problem?

   ☐ Yes ☐ No ☐ Unsure ☐ Unwilling to say

   Explain why you answered this way? _____
   _____
   _____

2. Write Your Title for Problem #2: _____

   What is the relationship between Problem #2 and your use of alcohol or other drugs?

   A. Did using alcohol or other drugs cause this problem? (Would you have this problem if you never used alcohol or other drugs?)

   ☐ Yes ☐ No ☐ Unsure ☐ Unwilling to say

   Explain why you answered this way? _____
   _____
   _____

B. Did using alcohol or other drugs make this problem worse than it would have been if you hadn't been using?

☐ Yes ☐ No ☐ Unsure ☐ Unwilling to say

Explain why you answered this way? _____

_____

_____

C. Did you use alcohol or other drugs to deal with stress or pain caused by this problem?

☐ Yes ☐ No ☐ Unsure ☐ Unwilling to say

Explain why you answered this way? _____

_____

_____

3. Write Your Title for Problem #3: _____

What is the relationship between Problem #3 and your use of alcohol or other drugs?

A. Did using alcohol or other drugs cause this problem? (Would you have this problem if you never used alcohol or other drugs?)

☐ Yes ☐ No ☐ Unsure ☐ Unwilling to say

Explain why you answered this way? _____

_____

_____

B. Did using alcohol or other drugs make this problem worse than it would have been if you hadn't been using?

☐ Yes ☐ No ☐ Unsure ☐ Unwilling to say

Explain why you answered this way? _____

_____

_____

C. Did you use alcohol or other drugs to deal with stress or pain caused by this problem?

☐ Yes ☐ No ☐ Unsure ☐ Unwilling to say

Explain why you answered this way? _____

_____

_____

4. **Denial Check:** Complete the two-part denial check below.

Part 1: What denial patterns did you use during this part of the exercise? (Check as many as needed.)	
1. **Avoidance:** "I'll talk about anything but my real problems."	7. **Compliance:** "I'll pretend to do what you want if you'll leave me alone."
2. **Absolute Denial:** "No not Me, I don't have problems."	8. **Manipulating:** "I'll only admit that I have problems if you agree to solve them for me."
3. **Minimizing:** "My problems aren't that bad."	9. **Flight Into Health:** "Feeling better means that I'm cured."
4. **Rationalizing:** "If I can find good enough reasons for my problems, I won't have to deal with them."	10. **Recovery by Fear:** "Being scared of my problems will make them go away."
5. **Blaming:** "If I can prove that my problems are not my fault, I won't have to deal with them."	11. **Strategic Hopelessness:** "Since nothing works, I don't have to try."
6. **Comparing:** "Showing that others are worse than me proves that I don't have serious problems."	12. **Democratic Disease State:** "I have the right to destroy myself and no one has the right to stop me."

Part 2: When did you notice you were using denial?

A. Not until after completing this part of the exercise and reading my answers.

B. While I was answering the questions.

C. I noticed the urge to start using denial before I started to answer the question, but I ended up using denial when I answered the questions anyway.

D. I noticed the urge to start using denial before I started to answer the question, and stopped my denial and answered the questions honestly.

Exercise 5-3: The Consequences of Continued Alcohol or Drug Use

1. Write Your Title for Problem #1: _____

   Think about this problem and answer the following questions:

   A. How could continuing to use alcohol or other drugs help you solve this problem or make it better?

   _____
   _____
   _____

   B. How could continuing to use alcohol or other drugs prevent you from solving this problem or make it worse?

   _____
   _____
   _____

   C. What is the best thing that could happen to this problem if you keep using?

   _____
   _____
   _____

   D. What is the worst thing that could happen to this problem if you keep using?

   _____
   _____
   _____

   E. What is the most likely thing that will probably happen to this problem if you keep using?

   _____
   _____
   _____

2. Write Your Title for Problem #2: _____

   Think about this problem and answer the following questions:

   A. How could continuing to use alcohol or other drugs help you solve this problem or make it better?

   _____
   _____
   _____

   B. How could continuing to use alcohol or other drugs prevent you from solving this problem or make it worse?

   _____
   _____
   _____

   C. What is the best thing that could happen to this problem if you keep using?

   _____
   _____
   _____

   D. What is the worst thing that could happen to this problem if you keep using?

   _____
   _____
   _____

   E. What is the most likely thing that will probably happen to this problem if you keep using?

   _____
   _____
   _____

3. Write Your Title for Problem #3: _____

   A. How could continuing to use alcohol or other drugs help you solve this problem or make it better?

   _____
   _____
   _____

B. How could continuing to use alcohol or other drugs prevent you from solving this problem or make it worse?

_____
_____

C. What is the best thing that could happen to this problem if you keep using?

_____
_____
_____

D. What is the worst thing that could happen to this problem if you keep using?

_____
_____
_____

E. What is the most likely thing that will probably happen to this problem if you keep using?

_____
_____
_____

4. **Denial Check:** Complete the two-part denial check below.

Part 1: What denial patterns did you use during this part of the exercise? (Check as many as needed.)	
1. **Avoidance:** "I'll talk about anything but my real problems."	7. **Compliance:** "I'll pretend to do what you want if you'll leave me alone."
2. **Absolute Denial:** "No not Me, I don't have problems."	8. **Manipulating:** "I'll only admit that I have problems if you agree to solve them for me."
3. **Minimizing:** "My problems aren't that bad."	9. **Flight Into Health:** "Feeling better means that I'm cured."
4. **Rationalizing:** "If I can find good enough reasons for my problems, I won't have to deal with them."	10. **Recovery by Fear:** "Being scared of my problems will make them go away."
5. **Blaming:** "If I can prove that my problems are not my fault, I won't have to deal with them."	11. **Strategic Hopelessness:** "Since nothing works, I don't have to try."
6. **Comparing:** "Showing that others are worse than me proves that I don't have serious problems."	12. **Democratic Disease State:** "I have the right to destroy myself and no one has the right to stop me."
Part 2: When did you notice you were using denial?	
A. Not until after completing this part of the exercise and reading my answers.	
B. While I was answering the questions.	
C. I noticed the urge to start using denial before I started to answer the question, but I ended up using denial when I answered the questions anyway.	
D. I noticed the urge to start using denial before I started to answer the question, and stopped my denial and answered the questions honestly.	

Exercise 5-4: Pulling It All Together

The purpose of this exercise is to help you pull together the information from the previous three exercises so you can look at the big picture of what is happening to you as a result of your alcohol or drug use and make decisions about what you want to do.

Review *Exercise 5-1* and list the problems that caused you to seek treatment in column #1: *Presenting Problems*. Review *Exercise 5-2* and describe how each problem is related to your use of alcohol and other drugs in column #2. Review *Exercise 5-3* and list the best, worst, and most likely things that could happen as a result of each problem in column #3.

1. Presenting Problems:	2. Relationship to Alcohol or Drug Use:	3. Consequences of Continued Use:
What are the presenting problems that caused you to seek treatment at this time?	How is each presenting problem related to your use of alcohol or drugs?	What will happen to your ability to solve this problem if you don't stop using alcohol and drugs?
Problem #1		*Best:*
		Worst:
		Most likely:
Problem #2		*Best:*
		Worst:
		Most likely:
Problem #3		*Best:*
		Worst:
		Most likely:

4. Review the information that you summarized on the previous table. Try to connect with what this information really means to you.

5. Do you think if you keep using alcohol or other drugs at this time your problems will probably get worse?

    ☐ Yes ☐ No ☐ Unsure ☐ Unwilling to think about it

    Explain your answer: _____
    _____

6. Do you think if you stop using alcohol and drugs, at least for a while, things might start getting better?

    ☐ Yes ☐ No ☐ Unsure ☐ Unwilling to think about it

    Explain your answer: _____
    _____

7. Do you believe it is in your best interest to stop using alcohol and drugs, at least for a while?

    ☐ Yes ☐ No ☐ Unsure ☐ Unwilling to think about it

    Explain your answer: _____
    _____

8. Are you willing to make a commitment to abstain from alcohol and other drugs?

    ☐ Yes ☐ No ☐ Unsure ☐ Unwilling to think about it

    Explain your answer: _____
    _____

9. Are you willing to develop an *Abstinence Plan* that will help you stay away from alcohol and other drugs while working to solve your problems?

    ☐ Yes ☐ No ☐ Unsure ☐ Unwilling to think about it

    Explain your answer: _____
    _____

10. Are you willing to be accountable for your decision to not use alcohol or other drugs by agreeing to participate in an alcohol and drug screening program?

    ☐ Yes ☐ No ☐ Unsure ☐ Unwilling to think about it

    Explain your answer: _____
    _____

11. Are you willing to start a treatment program that can help you implement your abstinence plan?

☐ Yes ☐ No ☐ Unsure Explain your answer: _____

_____
_____
_____
_____
_____

12. **Denial Check:** Complete the two-part denial check below.

Part 1: What denial patterns did you use during this part of the exercise? (Check as many as needed.)	
1. **Avoidance:** "I'll talk about anything but my real problems."	7. **Compliance:** "I'll pretend to do what you want if you'll leave me alone."
2. **Absolute Denial:** "No not Me, I don't have problems."	8. **Manipulating:** "I'll only admit that I have problems if you agree to solve them for me."
3. **Minimizing:** "My problems aren't that bad."	9. **Flight Into Health:** "Feeling better means that I'm cured."
4. **Rationalizing:** "If I can find good enough reasons for my problems, I won't have to deal with them."	10. **Recovery by Fear:** "Being scared of my problems will make them go away."
5. **Blaming:** "If I can prove that my problems are not my fault, I won't have to deal with them."	11. **Strategic Hopelessness:** "Since nothing works, I don't have to try."
6. **Comparing:** "Showing that others are worse than me proves that I don't have serious problems."	12. **Democratic Disease State:** "I have the right to destroy myself and no one has the right to stop me."

Part 2: When did you notice you were using denial?
A. Not until after completing this part of the exercise and reading my answers.
B. While I was answering the questions.
C. I noticed the urge to start using denial before I started to answer the question, but I ended up using denial when I answered the questions anyway.
D. I noticed the urge to start using denial before I started to answer the question, and stopped my denial and answered the questions honestly.

This exercise ends here. Take a break and get ready for your next challenge: Stopping denial as you think and talk about your life history.

Exercise #6: Stopping Denial as You Think about Your Life History

1. Significant Life Events:	2. Alcohol and Drug Use Pattern:
Describe the sequence of significant life events: Use brief bullet points that capture the essence of each event:	Describing the pattern of alcohol and drug use during each phase of the life line: Questions: 1. What substances did you use? 2. Quantity: How much did you use? 3. Frequency: How often did you use? 4. What did you want to get out of using alcohol and drugs? 5. What fears did you have about using alcohol and drugs? 6. What actually happened as a result of your alcohol and drug use?
Life Event #1:	
Life Event #2:	
Life Event #3:	
Life Event #4:	

1. Significant Life Events:	2. Alcohol and Drug Use Pattern:
Life Event #5:	
Life Event #6:	
Life Event #7:	
Life Event #8:	
Life Event #9:	
Life Event #10:	

3. What did you want alcohol or drugs to allow you to do that you couldn't do without them?
   _____
   _____
   _____

4. Did your alcohol and drug use get you what you wanted?
   ☐ Yes ☐ No ☐ Unsure Explain your answer: _____
   _____
   _____

5. What did you want alcohol or drugs to allow you to cope with or escape from that you couldn't when not using?
   _____
   _____
   _____

6. Did your alcohol and drug use give you the escape or coping skills that you wanted?
   ☐ Yes ☐ No ☐ Unsure Explain your answer: _____
   _____
   _____

7. After reviewing your history, what were the benefits and disadvantages that alcohol and drugs brought to your life?

Benefits of Alcohol and Drug Use	Disadvantages of Alcohol and Drug Use
1.	1.
2.	2.
3.	3.

8. What are the three most important things you learned about yourself by completing your history of significant life events and the relationship of those events to your alcohol and drug use.

   A. The most important thing I learned is:
   _____
   _____

   B. The second most important thing I learned is:
   _____
   _____

C. The third most important thing I learned is:
_____
_____

9. **Denial Check:** Complete the two-part denial check below.

Part 1: What denial patterns did you use during this part of the exercise? (Check as many as needed.)	
1. **Avoidance:** "I'll talk about anything but my real problems."	7. **Compliance:** "I'll pretend to do what you want if you'll leave me alone."
2. **Absolute Denial:** "No not Me, I don't have problems."	8. **Manipulating:** "I'll only admit that I have problems if you agree to solve them for me."
3. **Minimizing:** "My problems aren't that bad."	9. **Flight Into Health:** "Feeling better means that I'm cured."
4. **Rationalizing:** "If I can find good enough reasons for my problems, I won't have to deal with them."	10. **Recovery by Fear:** "Being scared of my problems will make them go away."
5. **Blaming:** "If I can prove that my problems are not my fault, I won't have to deal with them."	11. **Strategic Hopelessness:** "Since nothing works, I don't have to try."
6. **Comparing:** "Showing that others are worse than me proves that I don't have serious problems."	12. **Democratic Disease State:** "I have the right to destroy myself and no one has the right to stop me."

Part 2: When did you notice you were using denial?

A. Not until after completing this part of the exercise and reading my answers.

B. While I was answering the questions.

C. I noticed the urge to start using denial before I started to answer the question, but I ended up using denial when I answered the questions anyway.

D. I noticed the urge to start using denial before I started to answer the question, and stopped my denial and answered the questions honestly.

This exercise ends here. Take a break and get ready for your next challenge: Stopping denial as you think and talk about your addiction symptoms.

Exercise #7: Stopping Denial as You Think about Your Addiction Symptoms

This exercise will ask you to think about the most common symptoms that people have who are suffering from alcoholism or substance dependence. Notice what happens inside of you as you answer each of the questions. Does your stress go up? Does an inner conflict start? Do you feel an urge to lie or to tell partial truths? Notice what specific denial patterns go off in your mind.

1.	Do you use alcohol more than twice a week?	☐ Yes ☐ No
	Do you consider that a problem? ☐ Yes ☐ No ☐ Unsure ☐ Unwilling to say Explain: _____	
2.	On the days when you use alcohol, do you usually have three drinks or more?	☐ Yes ☐ No
	Do you consider that a problem? ☐ Yes ☐ No ☐ Unsure ☐ Unwilling to say Explain: _____	
3.	Do you use non-prescription drugs from time to time?	☐ Yes ☐ No
	Do you consider that a problem? ☐ Yes ☐ No ☐ Unsure ☐ Unwilling to say Explain: _____	
4.	Do you use prescription drugs that change your mood or personality?	☐ Yes ☐ No
	Do you consider that a problem? ☐ Yes ☐ No ☐ Unsure ☐ Unwilling to say Explain: _____	
5.	Do you sometimes use more than the amount prescribed?	☐ Yes ☐ No
	Do you consider that a problem? ☐ Yes ☐ No ☐ Unsure ☐ Unwilling to say Explain: _____	
6.	Do you get intoxicated on alcohol or drugs more than twice a year? (You're intoxicated if you use so much that you can't function safely or normally or if other people think you can't function safely or normally.)	☐ Yes ☐ No
	Do you consider that a problem? ☐ Yes ☐ No ☐ Unsure ☐ Unwilling to say Explain: _____	

7.	When you're not using alcohol or drugs, do you ever put yourself in situations that raise your risk of getting hurt or having problems?	☐ Yes ☐ No
	Do you consider that a problem? ☐ Yes ☐ No ☐ Unsure ☐ Unwilling to say Explain: _____ _____	
8.	Have you ever felt you should cut down on your drinking or drug use?	☐ Yes ☐ No
	Do you consider that a problem? ☐ Yes ☐ No ☐ Unsure ☐ Unwilling to say Explain: _____ _____	
9.	Have other people ever criticized your drinking or drug use, or been annoyed by it?	☐ Yes ☐ No
	Do you consider that a problem? ☐ Yes ☐ No ☐ Unsure ☐ Unwilling to say Explain: _____ _____	
10.	Have you ever felt bad or guilty about your drinking or drug use?	☐ Yes ☐ No
	Do you consider that a problem? ☐ Yes ☐ No ☐ Unsure ☐ Unwilling to say Explain: _____ _____	
11.	Have you ever done things while you were using alcohol or drugs that you regretted or that made you feel guilty or ashamed?	☐ Yes ☐ No
	Do you consider that a problem? ☐ Yes ☐ No ☐ Unsure ☐ Unwilling to say Explain: _____ _____	
12.	Have you ever used alcohol or drugs first thing in the morning to feel better, or to get rid of a hangover?	☐ Yes ☐ No
	Do you consider that a problem? ☐ Yes ☐ No ☐ Unsure ☐ Unwilling to say Explain: _____ _____	
13.	Have you ever thought you might have a problem with your drinking or drug use?	☐ Yes ☐ No
	Do you consider that a problem? ☐ Yes ☐ No ☐ Unsure ☐ Unwilling to say Explain: _____ _____	

Copyright © Terence T. Gorski, 2000. For books call 1-800-767-8181; (816) 521-3015; www.relapse.org.
For training or consultation call (352) 596-8000; fax (352) 596-8002; www.cenaps.com.

14.	Have you ever used alcohol or drugs in larger amounts then you intended? For example, have you ever used more than you wanted to or could afford to?	☐ Yes ☐ No
	Do you consider that a problem? ☐ Yes ☐ No ☐ Unsure ☐ Unwilling to say Explain: _____	
15.	Have you ever used alcohol or drugs more often than you intended? For example, have you ever planned not to use that day but done it anyway?	☐ Yes ☐ No
	Do you consider that a problem? ☐ Yes ☐ No ☐ Unsure ☐ Unwilling to say Explain: _____	
16.	Have you ever used alcohol or drugs for longer periods of time than you intended? In other words, have you ever not been able to stop when you planned to?	☐ Yes ☐ No
	Do you consider that a problem? ☐ Yes ☐ No ☐ Unsure ☐ Unwilling to say Explain: _____	
17.	Have you ever had a desire to cut down or control your use?	☐ Yes ☐ No
	Do you consider that a problem? ☐ Yes ☐ No ☐ Unsure ☐ Unwilling to say Explain: _____	
18.	Have you ever tried to cut down or control your use?	☐ Yes ☐ No
	Do you consider that a problem? ☐ Yes ☐ No ☐ Unsure ☐ Unwilling to say Explain: _____	
19.	Do you spend a lot of time getting ready to use alcohol or drugs, using, or recovering from use?	☐ Yes ☐ No
	Do you consider that a problem? ☐ Yes ☐ No ☐ Unsure ☐ Unwilling to say Explain: _____	
20.	Have you ever failed to meet a major life responsibility because you were intoxicated, hung over, or in withdrawal (having discomfort because you were no longer using)?	☐ Yes ☐ No
	Do you consider that a problem? ☐ Yes ☐ No ☐ Unsure ☐ Unwilling to say Explain: _____	

Copyright © Terence T. Gorski, 2000. For books call 1-800-767-8181; (816) 521-3015; www.relapse.org.
For training or consultation call (352) 596-8000; fax (352) 596-8002; www.cenaps.com.

21.	Have you given up any work, social, or recreational activities because of alcohol or drug use?	❏ Yes ❏ No
	Do you consider that a problem? ❏ Yes ❏ No ❏ Unsure ❏ Unwilling to say Explain: _____	
22.	Have you had any physical, psychological, or social problems that were caused by, or made worse by, your alcohol or drug use?	❏ Yes ❏ No
	Do you consider that a problem? ❏ Yes ❏ No ❏ Unsure ❏ Unwilling to say Explain: _____	
23.	Have you ever continued to use alcohol or drugs even though you knew they were causing physical, psychological, or social problems, or making those problems worse?	❏ Yes ❏ No
	Do you consider that a problem? ❏ Yes ❏ No ❏ Unsure ❏ Unwilling to say Explain: _____	
24.	Did your tolerance (your ability to use a lot of alcohol and drugs without feeling intoxicated) increase after you started to use?	❏ Yes ❏ No
	Do you consider that a problem? ❏ Yes ❏ No ❏ Unsure ❏ Unwilling to say Explain: _____	
25.	Do you ever get physically uncomfortable or sick the day after using alcohol or drugs?	❏ Yes ❏ No
	Do you consider that a problem? ❏ Yes ❏ No ❏ Unsure ❏ Unwilling to say Explain: _____	
26.	Have you ever used alcohol or drugs to keep you from getting sick the next day, or to make a hangover go away?	❏ Yes ❏ No
	Do you consider that a problem? ❏ Yes ❏ No ❏ Unsure ❏ Unwilling to say Explain: _____	
27.	When you use alcohol or drugs, what do you want those substances to do for you that you believe you can't do without them? _____ _____	
28.	When you use alcohol or drugs, what do you want those substances to help you escape from that you believe you can't escape without them? _____ _____	

Finding out What Your Answers Mean

1. How many times did you answer "Yes" to questions 1–13. _____
2. How many times did you answer "Yes" the questions 14–26. _____
3. Check the box below that fits your answers to question 1 and 2 above.
   a. **Low Risk of Addiction:** If you answered "No" to all of the questions.
   b. **High Risk:** If you answered "yes" to three or more of the questions numbered 1–13, and "No" to all of the remaining questions.
   c. **Early-Stage Addiction:** If you answered "Yes" to more than three of the questions numbered 1–13, and "Yes" to between three and six of the questions numbered 14–26.
   d. **Middle Stage Addiction:** If you answered "Yes" to more than three of the questions numbered 1–13, and "Yes" to between six and nine of the questions numbered 14–26.
   e. **Late Stage Addiction:** If you answered "Yes" to more than three of the questions numbered 1–13, and "Yes" to more than nine of the questions numbered 14–26.
4. You are probably dependent on alcohol or drugs and you believe that: (1) alcohol and drugs can do things for you that you can't do without those substances, or (2) alcohol and drugs can help you cope with things that you can't cope with unless you're using. Only people who are dependent on alcohol or drugs expect these substances to do things for them that they can't do without them.
5. **Denial Check:** Complete the two-part denial check below.

Part 1: What denial patterns did you use during this part of the exercise? (Check as many as needed.)	
1. **Avoidance:** "I'll talk about anything but my real problems."	7. **Compliance:** "I'll pretend to do what you want if you'll leave me alone."
2. **Absolute Denial:** "No not Me, I don't have problems."	8. **Manipulating:** "I'll only admit that I have problems if you agree to solve them for me."
3. **Minimizing:** "My problems aren't that bad."	
4. **Rationalizing:** "If I can find good enough reasons for my problems, I won't have to deal with them."	9. **Flight Into Health:** "Feeling better means that I'm cured."
5. **Blaming:** "If I can prove that my problems are not my fault, I won't have to deal with them."	10. **Recovery by Fear:** "Being scared of my problems will make them go away."
6. **Comparing:** "Showing that others are worse than me proves that I don't have serious problems."	11. **Strategic Hopelessness:** "Since nothing works, I don't have to try."
	12. **Democratic Disease State:** "I have the right to destroy myself and no one has the right to stop me."

Part 2: When did you notice you were using denial?
A. Not until after completing this part of the exercise and reading my answers.
B. While I was answering the questions.
C. I noticed the urge to start using denial before I started to answer the question, but I ended up using denial when I answered the questions anyway.
D. I noticed the urge to start using denial before I started to answer the question, and stopped my denial and answered the questions honestly.

**This exercise ends here. Take a break and get ready for your next challenge:
Stopping denial as you decide what to do next.**

Exercise #8: Stopping Denial as You Decide What to Do Next

1. What are the problems that caused you to seek help?
   _____
   _____

2. How is your alcohol and other drug use related to those problems?
   _____
   _____

3. Do you believe that you can successfully deal with those problems if you stopped using alcohol and other drugs, at least for a limited period of time?
   ☐ Yes ☐ No ☐ Unsure Explain your answer._____
   _____
   _____

4. Are you willing to make a commitment to get the help you need to stop using alcohol and other drugs??
   ☐ Yes ☐ No ☐ Undecided Explain your answer: _____
   _____
   _____

5. **Denial Check:** Complete the two-part denial check below.

Part 1: What denial patterns did you use during this part of the exercise? (Check as many as needed.)	
1. **Avoidance:** "I'll talk about anything but my real problems."	7. **Compliance:** "I'll pretend to do what you want if you'll leave me alone."
2. **Absolute Denial:** "No not Me, I don't have problems."	8. **Manipulating:** "I'll only admit that I have problems if you agree to solve them for me."
3. **Minimizing:** "My problems aren't that bad."	9. **Flight Into Health:** "Feeling better means that I'm cured."
4. **Rationalizing:** "If I can find good enough reasons for my problems, I won't have to deal with them."	10. **Recovery by Fear:** "Being scared of my problems will make them go away."
5. **Blaming:** "If I can prove that my problems are not my fault, I won't have to deal with them."	11. **Strategic Hopelessness:** "Since nothing works, I don't have to try."
6. **Comparing:** "Showing that others are worse than me proves that I don't have serious problems."	12. **Democratic Disease State:** "I have the right to destroy myself and no one has the right to stop me."

Part 2: When did you notice you were using denial?
A. Not until after completing this part of the exercise and reading my answers.
B. While I was answering the questions.
C. I noticed the urge to start using denial before I started to answer the question, but I ended up using denial when I answered the questions anyway.
D. I noticed the urge to start using denial before I started to answer the question, and stopped my denial and answered the questions honestly.

**This exercise stops here. Take a break and congratulate yourself.
The worst is over. All that's left is evaluating what you learned.**

Exercise #9: Evaluating Your Denial Management Skills

Instructions: The ultimate test of whether you have benefited from this process will be your ability to identify and stop your denial and start identifying and solving your problems. This evaluation will help you identify your areas of strength and weakness so you will be able to improve your overall skill at managing your denial.

Read each statement below and evaluate your level of skill before completing this workbook and your current level of skill after completing the workbook.

1. What did you want from completing this workbook?
   _____
   _____

2. How much of what you wanted did you get?
   ☐ All of it ☐ Some of it ☐ None of it
   Explain your answer: _____
   _____

3. What are the most important things you learned about yourself by completing this workbook?
   _____
   _____
   _____
   _____
   _____
   _____

4. What will you do differently as a result of completing this workbook?
   _____
   _____
   _____
   _____
   _____
   _____

5. The following questions will help you rate your skills at managing denial both before completing the workbook and after completing the workbook.

Skill #1: ***Understanding Denial as a Part of the Human Condition:*** I am able to explain why denial is a normal part of the human condition (*Exercise #1*).

- *My understanding denial as a part of the human condition:*
  Before: (0–10) _____ After: (0–10) _____

Skill #2: ***Understanding the Principles of Denial Management:*** I am able to explain the basic principles of denial management (*Exercise #2*).

- *My understanding the basic principles of denial:*
  Before: (0–10) _____ After: (0–10) _____

Skill #3: ***Recognizing Your Denial:*** I know the denial patterns that I tend to use most frequently and I can recognize when these denial patterns get turned on.

- *My skill at recognizing my denial:*
  Before: (0–10) _____ After: (0–10) _____

Skill #4: ***Managing Your Denial:*** I can stop my denial quickly when it occurs and focus on identifying and solving my problems.

- *My skill at managing my denial:*
  Before: (0–10) _____ After: (0–10) _____

Skill #5: ***Stopping Denial as You Think about Your Problems:*** I can stop using denial as I think about the problems that caused me to get help, how those problems are related to alcohol and other drug use, and what will probably happen if I keep using alcohol or other drugs.

- *My skill at stopping denial as I think about my problems:*
  Before: (0–10) _____ After: (0–10) _____

Skill #6: ***Stopping Denial as You Think about Your Life History:*** I can stop using denial as I think about my history of significant life events and how my use of alcohol or other drugs is related to those events.

- *My skill at stopping denial as I think about my life history:*
  Before: (0–10) _____ After: (0–10) _____

Skill #7: ***Stopping Denial as You Think about Your Addiction Symptoms:*** I am able to stop denial as I review the symptoms of addiction that apply to me.

- *My skill at stopping denial as I think about my addiction symptoms:*
  Before: (0–10) _____ After: (0–10) _____

Skill #8: ***Stopping Denial as You Decide What to Do Next:*** I can stop using denial as I think about what I need to do next to deal with my alcohol and drug problems.

- *My skill at stopping denial as I think about what to do next to deal with my alcohol and drug problems:*
  Before: (0–10) _____ After: (0–10) _____

Overall Skill at Managing High-Risk Situations: How would you rate the changes in your overall ability to recognize and stop denial quickly and refocus on identifying and solving your problems?

Denial Management Skill Level: Before: (0–10) _____ After: (0–10) _____

Why did you rate your changes in skill levels this way?

_____
_____
_____
_____

**This exercise stops here. Go to the next page.
We have some final words to share with you.**

A Final Word

Congratulations! You have now taken the first steps in recognizing the truth about what is happening in your life by learning how identify and manage your own denial. You can now choose to take the next step by developing a program of recovery. You can start using your new skills immediately to stop spinning your wheels by managing your denial and staying focused on solving your problems.

Many of you will find that once you learn how to effectively manage your own denial you will be able to fully recover by using your self-help program, counseling, and the denial management skills you learned. For some of you, however, these skills will not be enough. Some of you, especially those who were raised in a dysfunctional family, may need to go beyond denial management and learn how to identify and manage the high-risk situations and core personality and lifestyle issues that cause relapse. The relapse prevention processes that can help you do this are *Relapse Prevention Counseling (RPC)* for managing high-risk situations; and *Relapse Prevention Therapy (RPT)* for managing core personality and lifestyle problems. You can take this next step in your recovery by learning these RPC and RPT skills by completing the workbooks titled: *Relapse Prevention Counseling Workbook—Practical Exercises for Managing High-Risk Situations*; and *Relapse Prevention Therapy Workbook—Managing Core Personality and Lifestyle Problems*.

The challenge of recovery is never really over. It seems that once we start a recovery process we are either growing or we're dying. There is no standing still. We either commit ourselves each day to improving and refining our recovery skills, or we become complacent and slowly move toward meaninglessness, misery, and relapse. We must make a conscious choice each day about which path we'll follow.

As you move from completing this workbook to using your new skills in real life situations, remember that temporary setbacks may occur, but you can always choose to get back into recovery. *Recovery is possible.* By completing this workbook you have already taken a big step toward improving your chances of recovery and lowering your risk of relapse. Your next job is to use the skills you have learned in your day-to-day life and in your next formal steps in your recovery program.

If you get stuck anywhere in the process you can go to our Web site: *www.cenaps.com* and/or send an e-mail to *info@cenaps.com*. One of our certified specialists will be available to respond to your questions. Good luck on your personal journey! We're pleased and proud to have walked with you as you took your first steps toward recovery. Thank you for permitting us to do so!

> *Tomorrow Will be New Again*
>   *If We Have the Strength to Reach for Beauty*
> *And the Spirit to Pay its Price!*

—Terence T. Gorski & Stephen F. Grinstead

Appendix #1: Abstinence Contract

Developed By Terence T. Gorski   © Copyright, Terence T. Gorski, 1982, 1997
The CENAPS® CORPORATION   Phone: 352-596-8000
6147 Deltona Blvd., Spring Hill, FL 34606   Fax: 352-596-8002
Web site: www.cenaps.com   *E-Mail: info@cenaps.com*

I, _____ do hereby agree to the following terms and conditions of treatment.

1. **Abstinence:** I agree to ABSTAIN from using alcohol and mood-altering drugs as long as I am receiving service from _____. The term "drugs" as used here includes any prescribed or non-prescribed mood-altering chemicals (either legal or illegal) that I may use without informing and gaining the consent of my counselor.

2. **High-Risk Situations:** I agree to immediately tell my counselor about any problems or situations that may develop during my treatment that could cause me to start using alcohol or drugs despite my commitment.

3. **Cravings or Urges to Use:** I agree to immediately discuss any cravings or urges to use mood-altering chemicals with my counselor.

4. **Desire to Stop Treatment:** I agree to immediately discuss any thoughts or feelings I may have about wanting to stop coming to treatment sessions or stop participating in other recovery activities such as self-help groups.

5. **Self-reporting of Relapse:** I agree that if I do start using alcohol or drugs I will immediately report it to my therapist. After reporting my relapse to my counselor the following will happen: (1) My current treatment plan will be immediately suspended; (2) I will be asked to complete a new evaluation to determine what treatment is necessary to stop the relapse; (3) I will be given a treatment recommendation (that may include referral for detoxification, residential treatment, or participation in a more intensive or extended outpatient program); (4) If I refuse the recommendation I will be terminated from treatment.

6. **Getting Caught Using:** I understand that if I am caught using alcohol or drugs before I report my relapse to my counselor I will be offered referral for immediate detoxification. If I refuse the referral I will be immediately terminated from treatment. If I accept the referral I will be allowed to set up a new screening interview. It will be my responsibility to demonstrate in that evaluation session that I recognize what caused my relapse and my attempts to hide it and that I am willing to make an honest effort to work on resolving those problems. I understand that because of the dishonesty involved in my attempts to hide the relapse, the treatment program will exercise a high degree of suspicion during this evaluation. It will be up to me to clearly demonstrate my motivation to and willingness to change.

7. **Testing for Alcohol and Drugs:** I agree to submit to drug screens on a random basis and at the discretion of the clinical staff. I understand that my refusal to submit to a breath, urine, hair, or other required test will be interpreted as an admission that I have been using alcohol or drugs but refuse to admit it.

I will consult with _____ staff regarding any medications prescribed to me by a physician.

_____   _____
Signature of Client   Date

_____   _____
Signature of Witness   Date   (Revised March 22, 1988)

Appendix #2: DMC Model Treatment Plan

Developed By Terence T. Gorski © Copyright, Terence T. Gorski, 1982, 1997
The CENAPS® CORPORATION Phone: 352-596-8000
6147 Deltona Blvd., Spring Hill, FL 34606 Fax: 352-596-8002
Web site: www.cenaps.com E-Mail: info@cenaps.com

1. **Problem Title:** Severe Denial
2. **Problem Description:** The client is exhibiting strong denial of substance abuse and strong resistance to participating in treatment despite having serious alcohol- or drug-related problems.
3. **Goal**: The client will learn to recognize and stop the denial, recognize the problems with alcohol and other drug use, and accept appropriate recommendations for further help.

  • *Start Date:* *Target Date:* *Actual Date:*

4. **Interventions:** The client will participate in a combination of group therapy, individual therapy, psychoeducation sessions, supervised study halls, and self-help group meetings, in which the following interventions will be implemented:

    (A) **Understanding Denial as a Normal Part of the Human Condition:** The client will be able to explain: (1) That denial is a normal and natural response to experiencing serious life problems; and (2) that even though most people try to be honest, their human tendencies to make mistakes and then to lie to themselves and others about those mistakes can lead to the habitual use of denial.

    The client will achieve this understanding by completing and clinically processing a four-part exercise: *Exercise 1-1:* The Need to Search for the Truth; *Exercise 1-2:* The Tendency to Make Mistakes; *Exercise 1-3:* The Tendency to Lie to Ourselves; *Exercise 1-4:* The Tendency to Lie to Others; Exercise 1-5: Denial as a Normal Defense Against Pain.

    Level of Completion: ❑ Full ❑ Partial ❑ None *Completion Score (0–10):* _____
    Notes: _____

    (B) **Understanding the Principles of Denial Management:** The client will be able to explain: (1) That there are benefits and disadvantages to using denial and that the benefits can keep people using denial despite the problems caused by the disadvantages; (2) That acceptance and problem solving are antidotes for denial; (3) Denial can be defined in a way that can help people learn how to manage it; (4) The feelings that drive denial can be managed.

    The client will achieve this understanding by completing and clinically processing a four-part exercise: *Exercise 2-1:* The Benefits and Disadvantages to Using Denial; *Exercise 2-2:* Acceptance and Problem Solving as Antidotes for Denial; *Exercise 2-3:* Denial Can Be Recognized and Managed; *Exercise 2-4:* Defining Denial in a Way that Can Help Manage It; *Exercise 2-5:* The Feelings that Drive Denial.

    Level of Completion: ❑ Full ❑ Partial ❑ None *Completion Score (0–10):* _____
    Notes: _____

    (C) **Recognizing Denial:** The client will recognize the preferred denial patterns that are being used to avoid recognizing and accepting they have serious problems with alcohol and other drugs.

    The client will achieve this understanding by completing and clinically processing a six-part exercise: *Exercise 3-1:* Reviewing the *Denial Pattern Checklist*, *Exercise 3-2:* Learning How to Personalize Denial Patterns; *Exercise 3-3;* Selecting the Denial Patterns You Tend to Use; *Exercise 3-4:* Personalizing the First Denial Pattern; *Exercise 3-5:* Personalizing the Second Denial Pattern; and *Exercise 3-6:* Personalizing the Third Denial Pattern.

    Level of Completion: ❑ Full ❑ Partial ❑ None *Completion Score (0–10):* _____
    Notes: _____

(D) **Managing Denial:** The client will learn how to identify and stop using their preferred denial patterns by learning how to recognize when their denial patterns are turned on; recognizing the thoughts, feelings, urges, actions, and social reactions related to each denial pattern; and learning to use new ways of thinking. Managing feelings and urges, acting, and reacting in social situations that will stop denial and focus on recognizing and solving problems.

The client will learn to manage denial by completing and clinically processing a four-part exercise: *Exercise 4-1:* Managing the First Denial Pattern You Selected; *Exercise 4-2:* Managing the Second Denial Pattern You Selected; *4-3:* Managing the Third Denial Pattern You Selected; *4-1:* Bringing Your Denial Management Skills Together.

Level of Completion: ❏ Full ❏ Partial ❏ None   *Completion Score (0–10):* _____

Notes: _____

(E) **Stopping Denial as You Think about Your Problems:** The client will learn how to manage the denial patterns that are activated by thinking and talking about the problems that caused them to seek help.

The client will do this by completing and clinically processing a four-part exercise: *Exercise 5-1:* The Problems that Caused You to Seek Help; *Exercise 5-2:* The Relationship of Your Problems to Alcohol and Drug Use; *Exercise 5-3:* The Consequences of Continued Alcohol or Drug Use; and *Exercise 5-1:* Pulling It All Together.

The client will then complete a *Denial Check* to identify any denial patterns they used while completing the exercise and how long it took for them to notice when the denial pattern was turned on.

Level of Completion: ❏ Full ❏ Partial ❏ None   *Completion Score (0–10):* _____

Notes: _____

(F) **Stopping Denial as You Think about Your Life History:** The client will learn how to manage the denial patterns that are activated by writing a sequence of significant life events; describing the relationship of alcohol and other drug use to each of the events, identifying the anticipated benefits of substance use during each phase (What did the client want alcohol and drugs to do that he or she couldn't do without it); completing a cost benefit analysis on the actual outcomes of substance use (Did you get what you want? Was it worth the price?).

The client will then complete a *Denial Check* to identify any denial patterns they used while completing the exercise and how long it took for them to notice when the denial pattern was turned on.

Level of Completion: ❏ Full ❏ Partial ❏ None   *Completion Score (0–10):* _____

Notes: _____

(G) **Stopping Denial as You Think about Your Addiction Symptoms:** The client will learn how to manage the denial patterns that are activated by reviewing an *Addiction Symptom Checklist*; comparing the answers given to information provided during the *Life and Addiction History*; and reviewing an interpretation of the results.

The client will then complete a *Denial Check* to identify any denial patterns they used while completing the exercise and how long it took for them to notice when the denial pattern was turned on.

Level of Completion: ☐ Full ☐ Partial ☐ None   *Completion Score (0–10):* _____

(H) **Stopping Denial as You Decide What to Do Next:** The client will learn how to manage the denial patterns that are activated by making a conscious decision about what to do next to deal with their alcohol and drug related problems.

The client will then complete a *Denial Check* to identify any denial patterns they used while completing the exercise and how long it took for them to notice when the denial pattern was turned on.

Level of Completion: ☐Full ☐Partial ☐None   *Completion Score (0–10):* _____

Notes: _____

(I) **Evaluating Your Denial Management Skills:** The client will evaluate their denial management skills both before and after completing and clinically processing the exercises in the *Denial Management Counseling Workbook*.

Overall Level of Completion: ☐ Full ☐Partial ☐ None   *Completion Score (0–10):* _____

Notes: _____

_____

_____

_____

_____

_____

_____

_____

DENIAL MANAGEMENT COUNSELING
PROFESSIONAL GUIDE
Advanced Clinical Skills for Motivating Substance Abusers to Recover
By Terence T. Gorski with Stephen F. Grinstead

Project Team: *Terence T. Gorski, Stephen F. Grinstead, Arthur B. Trundy, Joseph E. Troiani, and Roland F. Williams*

This professional guide discusses a number of issues related to motivating clients to recover by using a systematic process to manage denial, overcome treatment resistance, identify serious problems, and motivate clients to resolve them. It includes:

Part I: Understanding Denial
1. Learning the Denial Management Systems
2. The Definition of Denial
3. The Levels of Denial
4. Denial and the Human Condition
5. Principles that Govern Denial
6. The Denial Patterns

Part II: Managing Denial
1. Confrontation in the Management of Denial
2. The Denial Management Interactional Process (A Communication System for Stopping Denial)
3. The Denial Management Clinical Exercises (How to Use the Client Workbook in Group and Individual Therapy)
4. Denial Self-Management Training (A Psychoeducation Program for Denial Management.)

Part III: Advanced Clinical Skills for Denial Management
1. Avoidance
2. Absolute Denial
3. Minimizing
4. Rationalizing
5. Blaming
6. Comparing
7. Compliance
8. Manipulating
9. Flight into Health
10. Recovery By Fear
11. Strategic Hopelessness
12. Democratic Disease State

ISBN 10: 0-8309-0965-6
ISBN 13: 978-0-8309-0965-0

To Order: Herald House/Independence Press
1-800-767-8181 or (816) 521-3015; *www.relapse.org*

For Training and Certification: The CENAPS Corporation (352) 596-8000; *www.cenaps.com*

Notes